Student Protest and the Technocratic Society: The Case of ROTC

by

Jack Nusan Porter, Ph.D.

"A lively penetrating history of radical politics at a major university"

ADAMS PRESS
Chicago

ZALONKA PUBLICATIONS
2912 N. 50 Street
Milwaukee, Wisconsin 53210

The author expresses his gratitude for permission to reprint the following copyrighted material: *The Daily Northwestern* newspaper, September 22, 1970, p. 6, "Orientation—Two Years Later."

Copyright © 1971, 1973 by Jack Nusan Porter

Library of Congress Catalog Card Number 72-97107

This is a shorter revised version of the author's Ph.D. dissertation, Northwestern University Library, June 1971, entitled "Student Protest, University Decision-Making, and the Technocratic Society; The Case of ROTC." Copies can be obtained from University Microfilms, 300 North Zeeb Road, Ann Arbor, Michigan 48106.

FOR THE YOUTH OF AMERICA, both in age and in spirit

> This means we must subject the machine—technology—to control and cease despoiling the earth and filling people with goodies merely to make money. The search of the young today is more specific than the ancient search for the Holy Grail. The search of the youth today is for ways and means to make the machine—and the vast bureaucracy of the corporation state and of government that runs that machine—the servant of man.
>
> That is the revolution that is coming.
>
> That revolution—now that the people hold the residual powers of government—need not be a repetition of 1776. It could be a revolution in the nature of an explosive political regeneration. It depends on how wise the Establishment is. If, with its stockpile of arms, it resolves to suppress the dissenters, America will face, I fear, an awful ordeal.
>
> —William O. Douglas, POINTS OF REBELLION, 1970, pp. 96-97

> The spirit of the people is greater than the Man's technology.
>
> —Huey P. Newton, 1968

> It riles them to believe
> that you perceive
> the web they weave
> And keep on thinking free.
>
> —The Moody Blues from
> "On the Threshhold of a Dream"

TABLE OF CONTENTS

List of Tables and Diagrams iv
Acknowledgements v
Preface vii
Introduction: The Transformed University 1

CHAPTER
   I. THE SETTING 9
  II. THE HISTORY OF POLITICAL ACTIVISM
      AT NORTHWESTERN 41
 III. THE HISTORY OF ROTC PROTEST, 1968-1970 57
 IV. THE NORTHWESTERN STUDENT STRIKE 75
  V. ROTC: PRO AND CON 91
 VI. ROTC AS TECHNOCRATIC SYMBOL 107
VII. EPILOGUE: BEYOND THE PROTEST 121

LIST OF TABLES

TABLE
1. Faculty by Schools 27
2. Highest Paying Institutions in United States 28
3. Percent Faculty Holding Doctorates by School 28
4. Student Referendum Compared to Questionnaire 94
5. Attitudes Toward ROTC by the Political Views
   of NU Students 95
6. Attitudes Toward NROTC Seen Longitudinally 124

LIST OF DIAGRAMS

DIAGRAM
1. The University as Corporation 12
2. Organizational Chart 21
3. Faculty Organization 33
4. University Influence and Decision Making 37

ACKNOWLEDGMENTS

This study could not have been accomplished without the help of many people. The intellectual and social debts that have accumulated are not always easy to pin down. Thanks initially must go to the following people for particular help in collecting the data and its analysis: Nan Hunter, Mary Pendergast, Sandy Smith, Kathy Shwerner, and Karen Wexler. To get all sides to the story, I had to interview many people. From Northwestern University's Associated Student Government, I thank Eva Jefferson and Mike Place; from ROTC, Col. Frank Gibson and Frank Haas; from Young Americans for Freedom (YAF), John Jensen and Robert Ritholz; from Students for a Democratic Society (SDS), I thank Paul Greenberg, Steve Lubet, Jeff Rice, and Ed Steinhart. Finally, I acknowledge my gratitude to the editor, Elliot Brown, and the staff of the school paper—*The Daily Northwestern,* particularly, Phil Lentz, Milt Politzer, and Mike Pollock.

The deans and administrators and their staffs have been extremely helpful, especially the past vice-president for student affairs, Roland J. Hinz, an academic "middleman" *par excellence;* the President of the university, Robert Strotz; and Jeremy Wilson of the department of planning for Northwestern. From the faculty, Richard Heflebower and Marvin Shinbrot, have aided my task immeasurable.

From the sociology department at Northwestern, my teachers and friends (not mutually exclusive categories) have been Bernard Beck, Howard S. Becker, Charles Moskos, and Jack Sawyer. At times, they may not even have known to what use I have put their knowledge.

My fellow graduate student friends, with whom I have shared many discussions far into the night, must include: Joe Blake, Wen-Lung Chang, Wally Handschin, George Kourvetaris, Barry Rozomofsky, and Jack Vastbinder.

There are also five people from outside the sociology department, I owe many debts: Sandra Acker Husbands, Karl Flaming, Howard Lorber, Edwarde "Buzz" Palmer, and Richard Rubenstein.

Finally, I must thank Robert F. Winch for providing needed financial aid to pay for the data collection and computer analysis, and to the members of my dissertation committee, Janet Abu-Lughod, Allan Schnaiberg, and Richard Schwartz, who amiably adjusted to a rapidly changing scene. Finally, I gratefully thank Deanna Rottenberg for typing the manuscript.

I think it would be apropos to mention the books and authors who have influenced my thinking and that have laid the foundation for this study: C. Wright Mills *The Power Elite* and *The Causes of World War III*; nearly any book by Paul Goodman, but in particular *Growing up Absurd* and *The Community of Scholars;* Herbert Marcuse's *One Dimensional Man*; and Theodore Roszak's *The Making of a Counter-Culture*. These books are essential to any understanding of today's unrest. Three important books that particularly tie together the universities, the corporate structures, and the military are William M. Birenbaum's *Overlive: Power, Poverty, and the University*; Seymour Melman's *Pentagon Capitalism;* and James Ridgeway's *The Closed Corporation*. All nine of these books, along with such newer ones as Charles Reich's *The Greening of America,* Alvin Toffler's *Future Shock,* and William Braden's *The Age of Aquarius,* all underscore the major issue of today: spiritual anarchy, political revolt, and personal malaise as means of adapting to the technological efficiency and dehumanization of post-industrial nations.

Oh yes, I must add four more people who have shared the tribulations and joys of this project: my father and mother, sister and brother. They finally got the "naches" they always wanted and so richly deserve.

JACK NUSAN PORTER
Milwaukee, Wisc.
Nov. 7, 1972

PREFACE

Students are really frightening. The following story should suffice. During my first year in graduate school in order to make some extra money, I taught "Sunday school" on Saturday at a synogogue in Evanston, Illinois. One spring, I thought to try something innovative, and I asked the class to write a poem about God and nature and the religious experience. I thought it would be a nice idea since *my* teachers had once made *me* do it, and I thought I'd attempt the same thing. Well, the students (all of them sweet young nine and ten years olds) were busy scribbling away, when one tiny little girl in granny glasses and a mini-skirt sidled up and asked: "Mr. Porter, do you want this poem to be in the style of Japanese Haiku with a 3-5-3 cadence and deal with *satori*, or what?"

I nearly fell off my chair. I thought to myself: doesn't anybody write about the robins and the trees and God in simple all-American rhyming couplets? Yes, the student is changing and he is frightening, and since I am, while writing this, still a student, then I too must be frightening . . . to someone. Revenge is an evolutionary process.

This story may symbolize in some small way what is occurring on campuses, and since that little girl will be in college one day, what is occurring today will accelerate in the future. The student arrives on campus, after having dined on 20,000 hours of TV and parental freedom, and finds an institution where he feels constrained, where teachers are afraid to lose the freedom to teach in the ways they've traditionally been taught, and where administrateors are afraid to share their power with students.

Most students plunk down their $4,000 to get a room and board, and accept it all, albeit grudgingly. They say: "What can we do?"—"You can't beat the system"—"anyway, education is a privilege, not a right," and then commence to toil away four, five, or more years for good grades, a degree, a job, and a "good" wife or husband.

That cycle lasted for a long time (and still continues), but some students somehow and in some ways decided to announce to the world what Herbert Marcuse calls The Great Refusal. They simply said—no! That small word stands like a rock with all of its devastating and delegitimizing force. Maybe Black people taught them the word; maybe the European or Latin American student; maybe ironically their own parents showed them the way. Whoever it was, when the word was finally given, the world was never the same again. Some say it started at Berkeley, refined at Columbia, honed at the 1968 Democratic Convention, sharpened at Cornell and San Francisco State College, and climaxed at Kent State University and at Jackson State University. These are all landmarks; who is next and what forms the protest will take is anyone's guess, but one thing is sure: The Great Refusal will continue far into this century.

The purpose of this study is to examine one portion of this Great Refusal—the history of protest, particularly that protest directed against the military presence of the Reserve Officers Training Corps Program, ROTC, at a prestigious, private Big-Ten school, Northwestern University. It will outline the course of that protest and its impact on faculty, administrators, and students. It will describe the various factions of student "subcultures"—the radical, liberal, and conservative. It will trace the history of ROTC protest from the very first "guerrilla theater" action in the spring of 1969 to the events surrounding the Kent State killings in the spring of 1970. It will examine the ideological pros and cons of ROTC, and finally, it will go beyond the rhetoric to examine why ROTC was considered a symbol of the entire technocratic society.

In short, protest, both symbolic and direct protest, must be seen not simply as a hit-or-miss attempt to rectify minor disillusions, nor as a clash between spoiled and pampered children and their authoritarian father-figures, nor as a short-lived description of the status-quo, but as an on-going, tenacious, even revolutionary quest for legitimization. To delegitimize the most dehumanizing and debasing aspects of the technocracy and to legitimate in their place new and creative alternative life-styles is the ultimate aim of student-Black-hip protest.

The entire issue of student protest somehow does not fit neatly into a sociological slot. It is not quite within the sociology of education though protest occurs within educational institutions, nor does it fit well within the realm of collective behavior even though it manifests certain qualities that might. It would be more productive to place it within the arena of political sociology, since, in essence, student protest like all of this past decade's protest has two aims: the redistribution of power and/or wealth and the alteration of consciousness. Thus, it is best seen as a direct political struggle for power and influence on one hand, and the introduction of a higher, transcendental form of reason on the other. It is a new consciousness that, according to Charles Reich in *The Greening of America*, will change politics, and, ultimately, the structure of society, by first changing the culture and the quality of individual lives.

It is by this "transcendental vision" that I have been guided. I do not claim to be objective in the narrow sense of that word, but I have attempted to back up nearly all my statements with facts, reason, and other scholar's data. Seymour Martin Lipset has said that in the case of student protest, it is almost impossible to separate one's role as scholar and citizen. Let me add that it is also difficult to separate, at times, the role of political pamphleteer and political sociologist. This book walks that narrow line.

Finally, it must be reiterated that the events described in this study are only minute catalysts. What is labeled an "apocalypse" at one point in time is merely a flash across the skies when seen from a distant historical perspective. By combining sociology, journalism, and history, I hope to examine that particular social "flash" known as student protest.

Introduction: The Transformed University

This country was founded by heretics. Its universities were founded by heretics. The "heresy" now found on our campuses had its precedents 350 years ago, and we've come around first circle. Protestant dissenters from England and Holland, many alumni of Oxford or Cambridge before being branded dissenters, were among those who landed at Plymouth Rock in the fall of 1620. By 1800, there were nine college institutions: Harvard (founded in 1636), Yale, Brown, Dartmouth, Pennsylvania, Princeton, Columbia, Rutgers, and William and Mary. They were mainly preparatory schools for the clergy; mathematics, speculative natural philosophy, Hebrew, Latin, Greek, and the classics were the "pith and marrow" of the curriculum. They combined the traditions of learning of ancient Greece, Rome, and Israel with the Christian Church with the demands and freedoms of the new world. The college of that time was a cloister for an intellectual and social elite, an aristocracy for the colonies.[1]

The university of today, however, is derived mainly from developments that arose immediately following the Civil War. The populist movement, the westward movement, the swirling rush of democraticizing forces set in motion by the sudden changes induced by the War between the States led to the rise of the university as we know it today. The community of scholars extolled by Cardinal Newman with its "pure" pursuit of knowledge was soon to be a nostalgic memory. Imitating the German model with its emphasis on graduate training, scientific research, and professional schools, a new form of education arose. Land-grant colleges were built by the Morrill Act of 1862; the first Ph.D. was awarded in 1861 by Yale; Northwestern University was founded in 1851 and awarded its

---

[1] For a more complete historical analysis of the university, see Stewart (1962) and Rudolph (1962).

first Ph.D. in 1896. Johns Hopkins was the prime example of the new graduate school universities. In the 1890's, the University of Chicago was founded, and it, along with Stanford, Columbia, and others, followed the "German model." National professional societies and journals were founded and knowledge was subdivided by departmental categories (i.e. history, sociology, physics, etc.), and the department emerged as the basic unit of academic administration. By World War I, two dozen major universities had emerged. An "academic revolution," as Jencks and Reisman (1968) have called it, was completed at this time, or at least the first round of it was.

If the first transformation of the American university occurred in the last quarter of the 19th century and dealt mainly with the professionalization of academia, the second transformation occurred during the after World War II, where the symbiotic relationship between the federal government and the university first bloomed. This "love affair" has intensified and continued up until this day.

Though there were efforts to restore the primacy of intimate "liberal education" with a stress on undergraduate training (mainly by Robert Hutchins at the University of Chicago), the mold, however, was set; the multiversity, the "closed corporation" as James Ridgeway calls it, became a reality. To aid the war effort, the collective minds of scientists and college administrators were needed. The "bomb" was developed under a tennis court at the University of Chicago. The innocence of academia was over; the newly emerged research-oriented, government-subsidized, IBM card-controlled multiversity was here to stay. Since World War II, the "knowledge explosion" has grown to enormous heights. About $2 billion was spent on scientific research and development in the United States in 1945. Today, the figure has risen to over $15 billion. Federal expenditure for research has multiplied 200 times in the past twenty-five years from $74 million in 1940 to $15 billion in 1965.[2] The post-war baby boom sent thousands of eager

---

[2] These figures are drawn from secondary sources discussed in Raymond W. Mack (1967:12).

students into the colleges of the land; the building boom constructed hundreds of new classrooms, dormitories and laboratories to house these students; the G.I. Bill and other federal incentives induced even more young people to seek college degrees. The armies of meritocracy were on the march. In 1900, only ten percent of college-age youth went on to college; now nearly sixty percent attend. If in 1900, there were nearly a quarter million students, by 1950 there were 2½ million, and today that figure has more than doubled to over six million students enrolled in the over 2,500 colleges and universities of the United States.

These educational institutions were caught by surprise. It is important to note that the Berkeley revolt of 1964 came exactly eighteen years after the "baby-boom" of 1945-1946. The stage was set for the third transformation of the American university. This new stage resounded from the small Catholic institutions of the Midwest to the Negro colleges of the South; from the sophisticated Ivy League schools of the East to the sun-drenched "surfboard" colleges of the West. What had happened was that in its rush to build and expand in order to accommodate the huge numbers of students wanting to get in, the university was forced to change. In their rush to build bigger and bigger universities, there arose indifference to the needs of students, and bureaucratic rules replaced human contact.

Along with the crush of over-population, there arose in the sixties other movements and events: the draft, the War in Vietnam, the Black protest movement, ecological problems, and the entire series of counter-cultures that opposed the meanest aspects of the growing technocracy. All these issues were, of course, developing over a period of years; it happened that in the 60's and now the 70's, they "bloomed."

It soon became clear that these forces of revolt and change developed dialectically in opposition to a growing phenomenon: the Corporate State. As Charles Reich has put it:

> Our present system has gone beyond anything that could be properly called the creation of capitalism or imperialism or a power elite. That, at least, would be a human shape. Of course a power elite does exist and is made rich by the system, but the

elite are no longer in control, they are now merely taking advantage of forces that have a life of their own. Nor is our system a purely technological society, although technology has increasingly supplied the basis for our choices and superceded other values. What we have is technology, organization, and administration out of control, running for their own sake, but at the same time subject to manipulation and profiteering by the power interests of our society for their own non-human needs. (1970:88-89)

In this Corporate State, the universities, or at least the largest and/or most prestigious of them, find themselves "deputized," that is linked into the military-industrial complex that lies at the foundation of the technocratic society. The government hires "private" firms to build national defense systems, to supply the space program, to construct the interstate highway system, to do research, and to train its military personnel (ROTC). We call these "private" firms by various names—corporations, research and development institutes, foundations, "think tanks," or universities; they are no longer separate and autonomous units, but are tied in directly to the Corporate State.

It is not that this situation is inherently cause for protest, but the very institution that many students (and faculty) felt was an autonomous and moral institution—the university—was ensconced within this Corporate State and contributed to those aspects of the relationship that were most abhorrent to these students: the WAR, military training, chemical-biological warfare research, etc. Thus the university itself becomes "part of the problem."

* * *

The focus of this book manifestly is student protest—particularly protest over the presence of NROTC, Naval Reserve Officers Training Corps, on the university campus. Yet the latent, and ultimately *the* most important issue, is not NROTC, nor the other campus issues, nor the radical's symbols, nor the "suicidal" acts of protest and confrontation—it is the *technocratic society* itself. The issue of NROTC or the war or oppression at home are only the most manifest symbols of the technostructure of post-industrial nations.

The issue of technocracy transcends the parochial and often narrow viewpoint of capitalism or communism; of liberal, conservative, radical, or revolutionary politics; of any left, rght, or centrist ideology. The issue of technocracy allows us to transcend such viewpoints, to see the historical and transnational effects, and to go beyond the restraints of the present. To view student protest as a response to technocratic pressures raises our horizons by merging the individual, his society, and his historical setting. Social scientists have too often concentrated on the psychological and the parental reasons for student protest, and have avoided intensively analyzing, or even mentioning, the technocratic. Yet it is both the psychological *and* the technocratic that cause protest revolt, and ultimately revolution. To avoid understanding the impact of the technocracy is to them view student protest in a piecemeal fashion—with little comprehension of the historical and macro-societal forces at work. One then misses the forest because of the trees.

Robert K. Merton, in his introduction to Jacques Ellul's excellent analysis of the technical civilization, *The Technological Society* (translated from the French: *La Technique: L'enjeu du Siècle*), has stated:

> By "technique," (one) means far more than machine technology. Technique refers to any complex of standardized means for attaining a predetermined result . . . Politics in turn becomes an arena for contention among rival techniques. The technician sees the nation quite differently from the political man: to the technician, the nation is nothing more than another sphere in which to apply the instruments he has developed. To him, the state is not the expression of the will of the people nor a divine creation nor a creature of class conflict. It is an enterprise providing services that must be made to function *efficiently*. (1964: VI-VII, original emphasis.)

It is the capacity to utilize techniques efficiently, to harness manpower effectively, and to employ deliberate and rationalized means which eventually become ends in themselves, thus replacing the very ends for which they were originally designed that is the *raison d'être* of technocracy. The era of expertise and of "know-how" is upon us, displacing the spontaneous, the inspirational, and the natural.

It should not then come as a shock that an entire series of counter cultures emerged during the 1960's to provide alternatives to the dehumanization caused by the technocracy. Whether one calls them hippies, or yippies, or revolutionists, or Black militants (the very terms are coined by the right arm of the technocratic state, the mass media), all are responses to the very same ethos: the technological and organizational imperative. I will, in this study, recount the activities of one of these "groups"—the radical left—but the very same technocratic repressiveness that the "left" fights against is also the one that the hippies, yippies, Blacks, and all other cultural and political insurgents fight against.

The "enemy" is not only powerful; he is devious. He is able not only to stifle, but to co-opt. He not only dehumanizes, but he "cools-out" his antagonists. The "new authoritarianism" (as Herbert Marcuse calls it) seems to be able to anabolize every form of discontent into its system. The technocracy is able to co-opt its dissidents, generate submissiveness, and weaken the rationality of protest. Such "repressive desublimination" (another Marcusian term) can undermine any discontent. Theodore Roszak gives the finest example, the sexual:

> To liberate sexuality would be to create a society in which *technocratic discipline would be impossible*. But to thwart sexuality outright would create a widespread, explosive resentment that required constant policing; and besides, this would associate the technocracy with various puritanical traditions that enlightened men cannot but regard as superstitious. The strategy chosen, therefore, is not harsh repression, but rather the *Playboy* version of total permissiveness. . . . Yes there is permissiveness in the technocratic society; but it is only for the swingers and the big spenders. It is the reward that goes to reliable, politically safe henchmen of the status-quo. Before our would-be playboy can be an assembly-line seducer, he must be a *loyal employee*. (1969:14-15, emphasis added.)

It is important only that the social machine, whether it be the corporation or the university, continue to roll onward and upward. All protest, no matter how irritating or embarrassing will be tolerated only so long as the vital machinery is left untouched. The dean of students at Northwestern University refers to his job as a "crisis-manager." He is correct. His duty is to see that crises are mediated and cooled-out, so that the machine can function with a minimum of disruption. The cry of "business as usual" during the Cambodia-Kent State strikes across the land in May 1970 was not necessary: the technocratic imperative is so powerful that by force of habit *and* design, universities would have returned to their pre-strike function anyway.

The reason that protest is seen both as a minor irritant and a major sore is that technocrats and their intellectual counterpart, the *academocrats*,[3] see such protest as essentially a temporary blockage of the technocratic dam, but know in the recesses of their mind that if such minor irritants are not dealt with effectively *today,* tomorrow they will swell and bring ever more complications. Furthermore, the technocrats are aware, albeit uncertainly, that the protest is *not* aimed only at an issue here or there, but that one's very life-style is also threatened, and moreover, the very function, role, and efficiency of the technocratic society itself is at stake! Again, Roszak (1969:16) says:

> We call it "education," the "life of the mind," the pursuit of truth." But it is a matter of machine-tooling the young to the needs of our various baroque bureaucracies: corporate, governmental, military, trade union, educational.

Since the radical critique of these institutions touches at a vital nerve center, the technocratic society is ready to do battle in order to protect itself. The purpose of this study is to articulate the history and sociology of this confrontation between a technocratic institution and the forces that oppose it. Suffice to say that this third transformation, the student revolt of the 1960's (and soon into the 1970's), is more than the transformation of only the academic institution: all the nooks and crannies of our society are its target. If academia has lost its "soul" and its "heart," so then have most societal institutions, and they all must be redefined. If the first transformation of the universities dealt mainly with pedagogic instruction,

---

[3] This term, which the author has newly coined, but exemplifies the role of the educator and educator-administrator who has "sold his soul" to the technocracy.

and the second transformation dealt mainly with national involvement, the third transformation deals mostly with moral principles. It is the search for a more human "community," a struggle for participation in the formulation of those rules and regulations that control one's life, a desire for "relevance" in all areas, a seeking of contact and compassion from teachers and office workers, an honest reappraisal of the university's involvement with non-intellectual (i.e. military) pursuits, an end to the myopic and deadening posture of academia, and a return to creativity, spontaneity, and love. If these demands seem naive and romantic, the response to them has nevertheless led to confrontations of fire and blood. Let us now begin to examine the setting for one of these "confrontations."

REFERENCES

Ellul, Jacques. *The Technological Society.* New York: Random House, 1964.

Jencks, Christopher and David Reisman. *The Academic Revolution.* New York: Doubleday. 1968.

Mack, Raymond W. *Transforming America: Patterns of Social Change.* New York: Random House. 1967.

Reich, Charles. *The Greening of America.* New York: Random House, 1970.

Roszak, Theodore. *The Making of a Counter Culture: Reflections on the Technocratic Society and its Youthful Opposition.* New York: Doubleday (Anchor Books), 1969.

Rudolph, Frederick. *The American College and University: A History.* New York: Alfred A. Knopf, 1962.

Stewart, Campbell. "The Place of Higher Education in a Changing Society." Pp. 894-939 in Nevitt Sanford (ed.). *The American College.* New York: John Wiley, 1962.

Chapter I
The Setting

The setting of this historical study is Northwestern University (hereon referred to as NU). It has two campuses, one in Evanston, a suburb north of Chicago, and one in the city of Chicago. The larger campus, located on a 169-acre tract along Lake Michigan, is called the Evanston Campus. Twelve miles south, on a 14-acre site just north of the downtown business center of Chicago is the Chicago Campus of the university. Buildings on the Chicago Campus house the Medical and Dental Schools, the School of Law, the Graduate School of Management, the Evening Division, and hospitals which are members of the Northwestern University Medical Center. The Evanston Campus houses the undergraduate and graduate students of the College of Arts and Sciences, the School of Education, Medill School of Journalism, School of Music, School of Speech, Summer Sessions, and the Technological Institute. The research on this paper took place on the Evanston Campus.

NU was founded in 1851 with a charter grant approved by the State of Illinois, thus marking a successful conclusion of the efforts of a Dr. John Evans (after whom the adjoining suburb of Evanston was named) and eight co-founders. It was the first private university to take permanent root alongside Lake Michigan, and it was an outgrowth of the pioneering spirit of the old Northwest Territory of the 1850's. The university is located in a suburb which also has the distinction of being the home of the Women's Christian Temperance Union (WCTA), whose founder, Francis Willard, was the school's first Dean of Women. To this day, Evanston is "dry." It has no bars nor liquor stores, or even a bowling alley.

NU was founded by Methodists, and its early students were Methodist ministers and students.[1] The first woman was admitted eighteen years later in 1869. Originally an undergraduate university, NU was among the first to offer professional (Medicine, Law, and Dentistry) and graduate education (Speech, Business Management, Engineering, and Education). In 1895, NU became a founding member of the Western Conference, the Big Ten of Midwestern Schools, and still remains the only private university in the Big Ten Conference. In 1896, it awarded its first Ph.D. degree. The school's growth coincided with the rise of the Chicago metropolitan area and today numbers 9,793 students on the Evanston Campus and 6,941 on the Chicago Campus.[2] This study will generalize only about the students and events of the Evanston Campus.

Though many would like to see it labeled the "Harvard of the Midwest," NU has long held the title of the "Country Club of the North Shore (of Chicago)."[3] A salient characteristic of this institution was its tradition as being a "finishing school" for the children of the corporate elite. The fact that students generally came from the upper-middle class and upper class and its high tuition and large Greek fraternity system added to this image. The image is rapidly changing as this dissertation will show, yet NU has never been known as a "hot-bed" of student revolt like Berkeley, Columbia, or the University of Wisconsin. Protest came later to NU than other schools, yet earlier than to some. On the activist scale, it stands somewhere in the middle.

This is not to say that NU is a "party school." Far from that; academically, it ranks very high among both private and public universities. In fact, it is quite underrated even by its

---

[1] For nearly 75 years, the sons and daughters of Methodist ministers paid reduced tuition.

[2] These figures reflect the fall 1968 report of *Northwestern University, Facts—1969* (1969). For a complete chart describing Northwestern students, see the next chapter.

[3] A better title would be the "Stanford of the Midwest," yet as one NU administrator said he hoped one day it would be the reverse —that Stanford would one day be the "Northwestern of the West."

own students and faculty. According to the U.S. Office of Education,[4] NU ranks (among private schools) fifteenth in the number of four-year bachelor's degrees awarded, eleventh in master's degrees, eighth in first professional degrees, and ninth in doctoral degrees. According to a well-known study in the evaluation of graduate education, the Cartter report, Northwestern ranks tenth in the nation among private schools and seventeenth in the nation among both public and private schools.[5] Assessing quality of universities is full of pitfalls. "Quality," says Allan Cartter, "is an elusive attribute, not easily subjected to measurement."[6] But by any "objective" measures NU ranks very high. Objective criteria plus subjective "image" combine to assess the rank of schools in the eye of the public, and NU ranks high on objective standards and is quite underrated on subjective terms.[7]

THE ACTORS

The university, being a complex organization, is in reality a "federation" of many diverse groups which at times run at cross-purposes with each other. These include the board of trustees, the administration (chancellor, president, and vice-presidents), the faculty, the individual colleges of the university, and the various subcultures of students. All will be discussed. First, the administration will be described. Wherever appropriate, comparisons will be made with other schools. Northwestern's organizational structure is similar to other universities; it most closely approximates the private schools. Public state-supported schools differ essentially from private ones in their governing bodies and means of support.

---

[4] U.S. Office of Education, (1968).

[5] These averages were made by taking the mean rank of the rated quality of graduate faculties mentioned in Cartter, (1966).

[6] Cartter, (1966:4).

[7] Again it must be reiterated that there are many ways of ranking universities—size of library, number of full-time Ph.D.'s, the prestige of the faculty, plus a host of other standards. No single scale can adequately measure a school's rank and prestige.

THE TRUSTEES

As has been emphasized in the introduction, the university is basically a corporate structure and, therefore, manifests many of the techniques and rituals of any technocratic institution. In fact, certain governing bodies of some universities are even called corporations. For example, Harvard's governing board is called the Harvard Corporation.

The Board of Trustees of NU is a managing board similar in many ways to the board of directors of a corporation. The Trustees are a select group. A quote by the Chancellor of Northwestern, J. Roscoe Miller, is apt: "The role of the board of course is one of management. It (NU) is a big corporation." [8]

These same words could have been spoken by the president of any of the corporations of the technocratic society—General Motors, IBM, Socony Mobil, or Con Edison. The following diagram may show these similarities more succinctly:

Diagram 1
The University as Corporation

CORPORATION	UNIVERSITY
Board of Directors	Board of Trustees
President	Chancellor
Vice-President, Sales	Vice-President, Student Affairs
Vice-President, Operations	Vice-President, Business
Vice-President, Financial Treas.	Vice-President, Comptroller
Vice-President, Ex. V-Pres.	Vice-President, Planning
Vice-President, Personnel	Vice-President, Faculties
General Managers	Deans of Schools
Managers	Department Chairmen
Employees	Faculty
Product	Students

---

[8] Quoted in the *Daily Northwestern*, (October 31, 1969:11). Much of the material in this section is based on personal interviews and a series of articles that appeared in the October 31, 1969 issue of the *Daily Northwestern*.

The top half of this diagram was not concocted by the author, but was specifically described by an NU vice-president himself. Consequently, it can already be seen that conflict is possible when the consciousness of these technocratic managers, with their pursuit of fund-raising and economic operations, is called into question by the activist students of the 1960's and now into the 1970's. Of course there are a few major differences between corporations and universities according to the administrators interviewed:

   a. There appears to be more freedom of expression in universities; more freedom of speech since there is an awareness of the social implications of the university's motives. There are limits to this freedom of speech, of course.

   b. There is a different criterium of advancement in universities—not necessarily for administrators, but for faculty. For example, in corporations one advances because of expertise and value to the "boss." In universities, the faculty advances by publishing, research, and teaching. Administrators seem to advance in similar fashion in both universities and corporations.

   c. There is no need to make a profit in universities as one should do in corporations. One only hopes to break even —which is not always done in reality. Most universities run in the "red."

The Board of Trustees at NU is a business-orientated group which is quite homogeneous in background and outlook. There are four major points concerning the Trustees:

   a. The Board of Trustees is a self-perpetuating structure. The new members are chosen by a nominating committee comprised of members of the Board of Trustees, and such a committee usually seeks what an administrator called "men of wealth and influence," especially if such men can induce others to donate and can donate money themselves to the university. And if the most obvious shared characteristic of the trustee is their economic concern (of the 40 members there are five bankers, twenty-five company/corporation presidents or board chairmen, and three lawyers), then new candidates will probably be of the same stamp as their predecessors. There are several advantages to belonging to the board of trustees of a university such as Northwestern. One, it is a civic duty and garners prestige for an individual.

Two, it is an opportunity for business contacts and stock market tips; and third, it is an opportunity for leads for new business executives. Since NU's trustees are representative of some of the wealthiest and most influential men in America, they are certainly not likely to be extremely enthused over the prospect of violent protest. The themes of the Board of Trustees are "peaceful change," "legitimate channels," and the "business ethic" of unthreatened influence and money.[9]

b. The trustees are generally alienated from the NU Campus. In some instances, they are ignorant of issues that are quite vital to the Northwestern Campus. For example, only two trustees said they read the school's paper, the *Northwestern Daily*. One trustee had not heard of an important report by the Faculty Planning Committee called "A Community of Scholars" which announced long-range educational plans. Most have not visited the campus to sound out student and faculty opinion, unless one includes the Homecoming football games. Of NU's 40-45 trustees [10] (including 20 "life trustees" who no longer have voting powers) only two have been involved in any kind of educational endeavor, such as members of a board of education or educational foundation.

c. The board is a mirror of the corporate elite as described by C. Wright Mills.[11] The corporate elite is characterized by a deliberate group which works under common assumptions and with similar perspectives. The NU Board seems to exude what Mills calls "a kind of reciprocal attraction among the fraternity of the successful." The active board members are on friendly terms with one another; there are extensive overlaps in both the corporate, financial, and social aspects of their everyday lives. Many meet at each other's homes and at each other's

---

[9] For an excellent description of the business orientation of the nation's universities and colleges, see Ridgeway (1968), Rauh (1970), and Hartnett (1969:58-59).

[10] The trustees are a fluid group with members added and dropped every year. The figures change but it is generally agreed there are approximately 40 to 45 members with a seven-man board of officers.

[11] See Mills (1956) and Domhoff (1967) for a further elaboration of these power elites.

exclusive social clubs.[12] Another example, six trustees of former trustees sit on the board of directors of *one* bank—Continental Illinois Bank and Trust Company. Also of the ten largest profit-makers in Chicago business in 1968, NU trustees were corporate officers or directors for five of them: Sears, Roebuck and Company; Commonwealth Edison; Allstate Insurance; Inland Steel; and Continental Bank and Trust Company. The interlocking directorates and inter-related business ventures of the men on the boards would be quite intriguing to investigate.

d. Last, the trustees are quite homogeneous. No Black men or women serve on the board. Only one woman serves. Few Jews serve. There are no members under forty years of age on the board. There are no students, no faculty, no staff, and there are virtually no political figures, active military personnel, or religious leaders. (There are a few Methodist ministers, including a bishop, on the board.) Politically, the majority of trustees are moderates, neither conservative nor liberal, and most vote Republican. It is safe to say that these same criteria also describe the vast majority of trustees on campuses across the country.[13]

There are a few summary remarks and final questions to be answered. First, it is important to note the internal mechanisms of decision-making and recruitment for the board. Decision-making and change is usually slow, deliberate, and endlessly discussed in the thirteen trustee committees. The issues are mainly economic, rather than educational. One trustee put it simply, "The board simply gets money for the university. It's not qualified to map an academic program;

---

[12] For example many belong to Chicago social clubs such as the University Club, the Glen View Club, the Saddle and Cycle Club, the Casino Club, The Chicago Club, the Lake Shore Club, the Commonwealth Club, and others. Many of these clubs exclude Blacks and Jews and seem to be overwhelmingly white, male, Protestant, rich, and Republican. More research is needed on such clubs.

[13] For one of the few pieces of research on trustees see the fact-filled study undertaken by the Educational Testing Service, (Hartnett, 1969). It also supports the findings of the present research. For an earlier analysis, and still relevant, see Beck (1947).

fortunately, it doesn't try to."[14] In fact the board exercises less power than the university chapter provides.

The board has the following powers:

a. To appoint and remove all administrative officers including the chancellor, president, and vice-presidents.

b. To require students to comply with all published ordinances, rules, and regulations enacted for their control by the board. Recent years have shown a number of board-passed decisions over campus drinking, disruption or occupation of buildings and classes, and student parietals (male visitation hours).

c. To make and alter "from time to time" the bylaws that govern the university, as long as such by-laws do not violate state and federal laws.

d. To "take, hold, use, and manage, lease and dispose of (university) property . . ." In fact, there has been conflict over profitable tax-exempt property lease-backs as well as controversy over land in an adjacent Black area of Evanston.

There are other powers, but the major emphasis of the trustees is as a check against administrative decisions. In fact, since most duties of the board are economic and deal with issues such as fund-raising, budget, property, insurance, and planning, there is heavy reliance upon "obedient" and well-chosen administrators. Until the beginning of student protest in 1967-1968, the major role of trustees was as fund-raisers rather than policy-makers. Increasingly, the trustees, because of the exigency of student protest and alumni pressure, have begun to make more policy statements and has consequently put more pressure on the administrators to enforce such policy, thus faculty and students, down the line, have felt pressure to comply.

---

[14] *The Daily Northwestern,* (October 31, 1969:14).

There is a close working relationship between the Chancellor and the board, and the former is an intermediary, a middleman, between the board and the administrators, just as the vice-president for student affairs and dean of students is a middleman between the administrators and the students. Though the Chancellor is viewed as the "boss" to most students, he in fact is theoretically an employee of the university and his salary is paid for by the board. His "boss" is the board.

There is no question that boards of trustees, like the university generally, are changing as a response to student protest. Newer trustees are generally younger, more liberal, and more education-oriented than their predecessors. A few schools such as Princeton, the City University of New York, Lehigh, Vanderbilt, and the University of Connecticut have appointed trustees from the under-thirty rank. More Blacks, more women, more "third-world" members, more Jews, and more "activist" members are also being sought. Such changes bring fear and distrust from over-50 board members when seen as a gradual erosion of their power. The long range effects of such change will have to be seen. An important *caveat* about the "tricky" methods of co-optation used by the technocratic institutions in pacifying dissent is that appointing one or two young liberal voices on a forty-man board is really a means to pacify students with the image, *not* the reality of shared power.

Yet the major question is really who has the power in the university: It may be fine that trustees add liberal board members, or even a student (as may occur at NU), or even begin to visit campus and talk to students and faculty (as occurred during the Kent State strike on campus), but in the actual sharing of power, who will one share with? One of the difficulties in the technocratic society is *secrecy,* secrecy as to who makes final decisions and who has jurisdiction over what areas. Due to this secrecy, the common assumption is that the technocracy moves forward like a machine, efficiently guided but with no moral leadership at its helm. One trustee has stated: "Trustee power is more fancied than real. Actually it's the faculty that runs the university through its committees and departments. The chief power of the trustee is the power to ask the right questions—to push administrators, faculty, and students into making the decisions." [15]

The power of the trustees is overrated in some ways. They do *not* have power over *all* areas of the university—but they are a powerful influence and antagonist if decisions are reached that it may not agree with. For example, issues of protest over war stock and property is a trustee's issue. Protest over credit for ROTC and Black studies is essentially a faculty issue. Therefore, different areas are decided upon by different groups and not always is the aim as direct nor as accurate as it could be. The major power of any governing technocratic board is really not only what power it has, but what power *it has and does not use*. It is this "reserve power" to influence and coerce that is important and not always its utilized power. In short, however, one can say that over educational and curriculum policies, the faculty has most power; over economic issues and as a final check in "overall" university decisions, it is the Board of Trustees (especially a smaller internal côterie of decision-makers) and the Chancellor plus his administrators that have nearly all power. One additional point: private schools such as NU usually involve more administrators and faculty in decision-making plus there is more freedom of decision than at tax-supported state universities which are governed by politically appointed regents and where there is less autonomy —many decisions being legislated at the state and local level of government. Yet protest has struck at both public *and* private schools, both large and small, autonomous and compliant.[16]

THE ADMINISTRATION

The administration at NU (and it is similar to other schools) is composed of the following positions:
The Chancellor: The chancellor is the highest administrative position in the university. The present chancellor was inaugurated as the university's twelfth president in 1949. Thus, until

---

[15] The *Daily Northwestern*, (October 31, 1969:16).
[16] The same point is made by Becker, (1970:1).

recently the chancellor held *both* positions of president and chancellor. In 1969, a presidential search committee of trustees, faculty, and students was formed to search for a president and to make its recommendations to the Board of Trustees: after much deliberation, the former dean of the College of Arts and Sciences was selected as president in July of 1970. The reason for splitting these roles was that it was impossible for the present chancellor to handle both of them. The chancellor's duties had been likened by one administrator to the role of "outside man." He is involved with contacts with people of wealth in order to sustain the university economically. He helps raise money for the institution by going to such men of wealth, to corporations, and governmental agencies. NU, being a private school, depends on 44 percent of its support income to come from either stock investments, government overhead, and private or corporation gifts.[17] Thus, a great deal of his time is spent away from campus conferring intimately with the Board of Trustees and their Executive Committee. The chancellor had rarely, if ever, addressed a spontaneous crowd. In fact, nearly all students never see the chancellor until graduation day or Homecoming ceremonies.[18] A shadowy figure to most students (and faculty), he nevertheless wields much power. He meets regularly with his administrative vice-presidents, which form the Chancellor's Cabinet. (Also included is the University Attorney). The chancellor also meets with the 24-man Chancellor's Administrative Council which consists of the Chancellor's Cabinet, the Deans of the Colleges and Schools, the University Librarian, the Director of Athletics,

---

[17] For a more exact breakdown:

Tuition fees	$45,000,000	56%
Stock income	11,000,000	14
Gifts	14,000,000	18
Government overhead	10,000,000	12
Total	$80,000,000	100%

The stock income is derived from a stock portfolio valued at $220,000,000.

[18] One year, in 1968, this proved an embarrassment, when the chancellor had to bestow the traditional kiss on the homecoming queen. That year the queen was a black woman. Reports were that he didn't kiss her.

the University Attorney, and the Chief of Campus Security. (See Diagram 2.) The Board of Trustees elects the chancellor, president, a provost, and the six vice-presidents, each of whom is responsible for a major administrative area within the university.

Though these are the formal organizational structures, the informal structures of decision-making are more difficult to get at. It would seem that it is in the cabinet meetings, held daily, where the budget is discussed and where the day to day reports are given and decisions are made. Informally, the Vice-President for Planning and Development has quite a disproportionate amount of influence. One administrator states: "His job is most important; he's a very powerful man." Nevertheless, there is autonomy among administrators, yet like in all team efforts, one learns to call in help. Decisions are made in informal power groups with some administrators having greater influence than others.[19] Though elected by the trustees, the chancellor is seen as an equal and had close relations with the board, especially the President of the Executive Committee of the board, the most powerful man of the trustees.

The President: This post was filled in July of 1970. Because of organizational reshuffling in 1969, the president handled the university's internal affairs—faculty, curriculum, and large intra-university issues. If the chancellor is an "outside" man dealing more with fund-raising and meeting the men of wealth, the president is an "inside" man dealing more with educational policies and meeting with the academicans. He usually has greater contact with students and faculty.

The Provost and Vice President, Dean of Faculties: The provost and his staff work with deans of each college and school on campus handling appointments, salaries, and resignations of faculty members. While the faculty of each college controls degree requirements and curriculum, the question of salaries

---

[19] Again one must reiterate that it is difficult for most researchers, especially if one does not wear a tie and suit, to find this out. Secrecy among top administrators is rampant. Furthermore, there is a great lack of existing literature in this area. Most researchers have concentrated on students and faculty.

Diagram 2
Organizational Chart

Board of Trustees

Chancellor

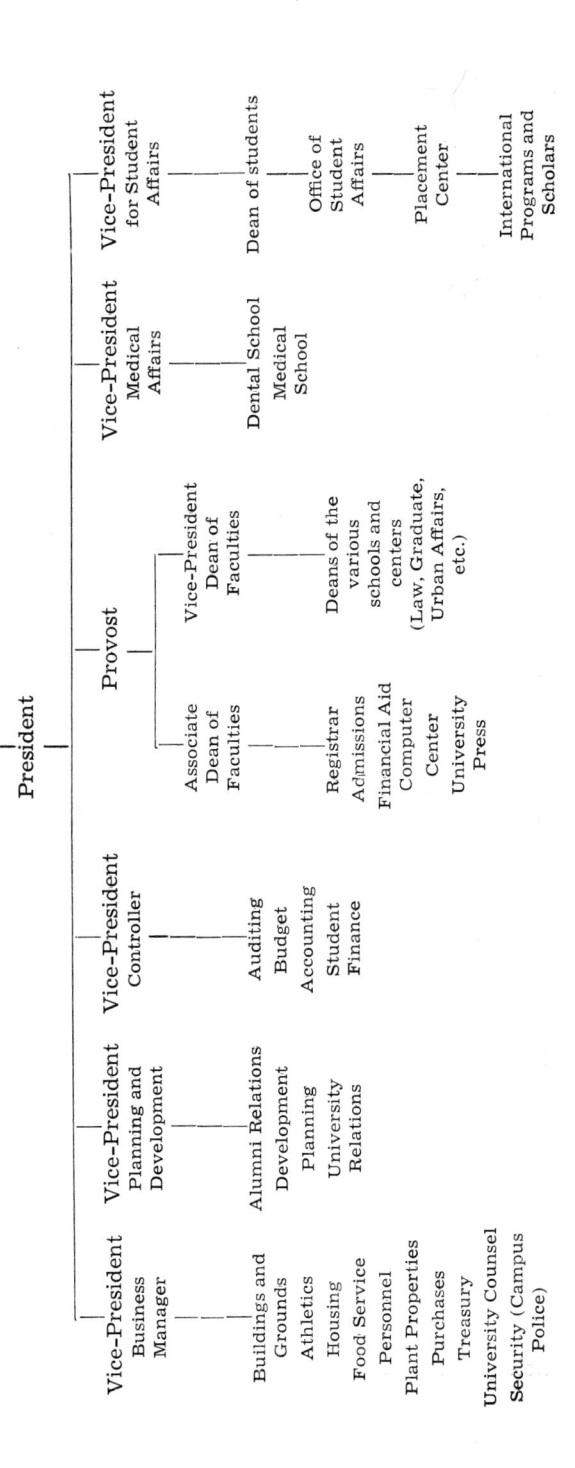

President

Vice-President Business Manager
- Buildings and Grounds
- Athletics
- Housing
- Food Service
- Personnel
- Plant Properties
- Purchases
- Treasury
- University Counsel
- Security (Campus Police)

Vice-President Planning and Development
- Alumni Relations
- Development
- Planning
- University Relations

Vice-President Controller
- Auditing
- Budget
- Accounting
- Student Finance

Provost

- Associate Dean of Faculties
  - Registrar
  - Admissions
  - Financial Aid
  - Computer Center
  - University Press
- Vice-President Dean of Faculties
  - Deans of the various schools and centers (Law, Graduate, Urban Affairs, etc.)

Vice-President Medical Affairs
- Dental School
- Medical School

Vice-President for Student Affairs
- Dean of students
- Office of Student Affairs
- Placement Center
- International Programs and Scholars

and appointments are the concern of the provost. The present vice-president is to retire in three years; a search committee was formed to investigate possible candidates for the position. As NU's chief academic officer, the vice-president investigates academic problems and coordinates the various school deans and faculty committees to solve them.

Vice-President—Planning and Development: The role of this position is in the area of long and short-range planning of both educational, economic, and building programs. This role also includes the coordination of fund-raising, alumni relations, and university public relations. There are large and separate staffs dealing with each of these areas. Its major duty is to gather financial support and to be an effective tool in the administration and management of "money, facility, and people." As was stated, the present role is filled by a man who by personality alone has moved up the career ladder and who has strong "hawkish" views on both protest and protesters. These views have made an impact on top administrative decisions with regards to these areas.[20]

Vice-President and Business Manager: The role of the business manager is strictly with the business end of the university, not the academic end. Such diverse issues as construction contracts, union rates, investments, food service, campus security, electrical work, and other similar areas are within this domain. It is a position not noticed by students nor by most analysts of the university scene, yet it is a most important area. "Our duty is to house, clothe, and feed the students; our job is to service this group of students," this administrator stated.

Vice-President and Controller: The duties of this vice-president is seen mainly as a C.P.A. for the university. His role is to

---

[20] The Vice-President for Planning and Development was recruited from the ranks of the police. He is the Chairman of the Chicago Police Board and a member of the International Association of Chiefs of Police. He is also a retired brigadier general in the Army Reserve, as well as the organizer of NU's Traffic Institute, which became a target of student radicals because it was a training center for policemen for across the nation. He has recently left NU to become president of the Automobile Manufacturers Association in Detroit.

serve as administrative accountant for the school. He works closely with the business manager.

Vice-President for Medical Affairs: This is a new position which was inaugurated during the reshuffling of 1969. The role of this position is to first, coordinate the administration of the university's medical and dental programs, facilities, research, and educational policies of the Northwestern University Medical Center which was formally incorporated in 1967. Secondly, it is concerned with the medical and psychiatric welfare of students and faculty on campus.

Vice-President for Student Affairs: This role which included the duties of the Dean of Students was split into two roles in 1969. One would deal with internal student problems and the other with larger issues of student-administrative relationship. This role and the staffs involved are directly concerned with student welfare—housing, fraternities, conflict-mediation, and the rules and regulations of campus life. The man in this role can be considered a middleman *par excellence,* whose job it is to mediate between student demands and administrative constraints. It is a difficult role—demanding, thankless, and filled with crises. It is this role which has played a prominent part in the student unrest on campus. Because of the great tension and strain that goes with the job, there is a fairly high turnover in job applicants. The Vice-President for Student Affairs is the major funnel of information about students to the administrators, the chancellor, and ultimately the trustees.[21] While it may be a vulnerable and precarious role, it is also a powerful one. Generally speaking, this position is filled by a man (or woman) younger than that of the other vice-presidents, and this person is more sympathetic and more knowledgeable about students than the other vice presidents.

Two other positions must be mentioned since they are also on the top decision-making governing boards—the Associate

---

[21] The chief of campus security police, which keeps dossiers on student militants, also aids in this task.

Dean of Faculties and the University Counsel.[22] The Associate Dean has jurisdiction over such areas as the registrar's office, the office of admissions, and certain other educational areas. The counsel and his staff of four lawyers is legal advisor to the university and assistant secretary to the Board of Trustees. His other duties are to handle all insurance policies for NU and to be in charge of litigation—the "inside" liaison man for the university with the help of the school's "outside" lawyers.[23]

In summary, it can be said that administrators are well-chosen and are well-rewarded. Most enjoy their work and spend ten to fourteen hours a day at it. There is both prestige and satisfaction from doing a job well. All the vice-presidents, except for the Vice-President for Student Affairs, are over fifty years of age. They have worked together closely (except for the new appointees) for over a decade or more and they trust each other's decisions. Their duties are two-fold: economics and image. They see their jobs essentially to keep the university solvent economically, and like those of all technocratic or academocratic managers, this job must be done efficiently and expertly. The image of the school is important not only because it is possible for a great school to be defamed, but because defamation is bad business. It effects not profits as in a corporation, but donations. For a private university, donations and subsequently alumni or other influence, is the "bread and butter" of the university. It is essential that neither be threatened.

---

[22] See Diagram 2 for NU's organizational chart. This chart must be read with the understanding that they can be misleading. The chart shows "up and down" relationships; much important interaction also is sideways. The chart does *not* show the informal power structure.

[23] He is also a rear admiral of the Navy Reserve. The chancellor is also a retired officer of the Navy. This is important to note now since this may explain (a) how and why NU acquired NROTC rather than Army ROTC, and (b) why there is sympathy for NROTC's position on campus. These two statements will be more fully discussed in a later chapter.

Therefore, when student protest arises, it has economic as well as political amplifications. An administrator's quote is apt here:

> "Take the damage to our buildings after violent protest occurs. It cost $3,400 to take the writings off those walls. We could use that money to repaint a classroom and insert new lighting, or something. The damage is a useless waste . . . and the violence done to property affects the businessmen who see it. They hear the stories and all they say is, 'Why can't *you* control those students?'
>
> "And this affects our fund raising. Why after the ROTC protest, some businessmen told us to see them next year! They won't donate . . .
>
> "Of course, we're entering also a period of tight money and inflation, but this kind of protest hurts us—right in the pocketbook."

This very honest and sincere appraisal points out how the political and the economic mesh. Protest is seen as bad not only in its own right, but in a business sense because it affects the economic structure of the university, and to a good businessman economics speaks louder than most other considerations.

THE FACULTY

The hidden "power" in many universities is, interestingly enough, the most visible—faculty members. Increasingly, one is convinced that a *united* faculty is the most influential component of the complex organization of the university, even more powerful than the administration or the trustees. One can ignore or suppress students, but with faculty members if this is done (and if the market is open), they will simply leave and the university suffers. However, two things mitigate against this "power": one, few faculties are united and unified either organizationally or ideologically over issues—especially of student protest, and two, few faculties have reached the political consciousness to understand the ultimate meaning of their power and influence. It is simply a matter of training and temperament. Faculty members has been taught over the years, especially through the socialization pattern of graduate training, that their role is to do research, to publish, and to teach. Other areas are to be left to administrators. As one vice-president stated in the course of an interview: "The dominant force in the university is the faculty—in academic areas. The economic areas are ours; faculty shouldn't have to bother with that area, (they should) devote their time to teaching and research."

This division of labor is based on the premise—"We won't tell you how to teach; you don't tell us how we should invest our money,"—underscores the historical relationship between faculty and administration. When this division of labor was threatened by the penetrating questions of activist students, the faculty member found himself in a cross-fire between his own professional and organizational loyalties and his moral commitments to students, and his own conscience. The best description of this "schizophrenia" is presented by Sklar (1970) who, incidentally, has done one of the few studies of faculty *qua* faculty involvement in student protest:

> "American academic communities, and as a consequence, American academic men, represent a curious mixture of freedom and constraint. Professors enjoy a fair degree of autonomy and despite the encroachments of legislative bodies and governing boards have a great deal of freedom in guiding not only their own professional lives but also the destinies of their institutions. As a result, when confrontation occurs, the academic man, because of the variety of his dispositions, interests, and commitments is likely to be torn by conflicting interests, sentiments, and loyalties. On the one hand are his loyalties to the institution; on the other his devotion to students, their radicalism perhaps reflecting his own concerns about the ills of contemporary society." (Sklar, 1970: 3-4)

It is not only a dilemma for professors to question their loyalties, but their *raison d'être* as scientists. What is the role of the scientist and citizen? What is the role of the scientist as a producer of social forces, as someone via his research and scientific work contributes to a reshaping of the social reality? What is the role of the scientist as colleague and teacher? What is the role of the scientist as participant in social action when these roles are defined by nonprofessional standards?[24]

---

[24] For a cogent discussion of these issues, from the perspective of a social scientist, see Kelman (1968).

These questions have been asked before by Max Weber, Robert Lynd, and Gunnar Myrdal, among others; and each generation of faculty members has been forced to reappraise its role and function. Yet who is the "typical" faculty member? Generalizations will be made cautiously. But first off, let us describe the organizational structure of the NU faculty.

On the Evanston Campus, there are 894 full or part-time faculty members.[25] For the 9,793 students on the Evanston Campus, this is a faculty student ratio of 1 to 11. By schools the break-down is as follows:

TABLE 1

FACULTY BY SCHOOLS

	Full-time	Part-time	No Stipend	Total
College of Arts and Sciences	391	36	15	442
Business	69	7	—	76
Education	34	13	2	49
Journalism	21	15	—	36
Music	50	28	—	78
Speech	58	2	—	60
Technological Institute	111	13	1	125
Transportation Center	27	1	—	28
Total Evanston	761	115	18	894

As per salaries, NU ranks as one of the highest in the country among all U.S. colleges and universities. According

---

[25] All statistics are from *Northwestern University—Facts 1969*, (1969:30-32).

to the American Association of University Professors (for 1967-68), NU's full-time faculty members earn an average of $14,838 for nine months' work. The highest paying institutions are as follows: [26]

TABLE 2

HIGHEST PAYING INSTITUTIONS IN UNITED STATES
(For 1967-68)

Harvard	$16,200
University of Chicago	16,057
Stanford	15,387
Johns Hopkins	15,281
California Institute of Technology	15,248
Hebrew Union (Ohio)	15,248
Northwestern	14,838
Claremont Graduate School and University Center	14,697
New School for Social Research	14,539

Of all full-time faculty, 76 percent hold doctorates. The breakdown by schools is as follows:

TABLE 3

PERCENT FACULTY HOLDING DOCTORATES
By School

	Percent
College of Arts and Sciences	80%
Business	79
Education	82
Journalism	29
Music	29
Speech	66
Technological Institute	91
Total Average	76% of full-time faculty

---

[26] From the *American Association of University Professors Bulletin*, (1968).

As for research, in 1967-68 Northwestern faculty members engaged in research projects amounting to $23 million, of which $19 million was government sponsored and $4 million by private and state sources. The faculty was engaged in that same year in some 1,000 research projects assisted by approximately 1,500 graduate students and technicians. Among private universities, NU ranked nineteenth in total federal support for 1967-68.

From this information, one can summarize that NU has highly paid and heavily-financed research professors. Yet it must be made clear that there is asymmetry here. Though the professors in the Technological Institute (engineering, astronomy, chemistry, physics, etc.) make up 14 percent of the faculty they have power over 83 percent of the research funds. This fact is true across the country and in all schools: money available to research and teaching of the technological and technocratic far outweighs that of the social sciences and humanities. This "cultural lag" is one of the major elements within the technocratic state.

There are social and psychological differences between faculty members possibly based on this "lag," by temperament, by training, and other factors. Yet, it is important to note that these differences are changing. For example, traditionally, most liberal and nearly all radical professors are social scientists (with a high number of sociologists and psychologists) and from the humanities (Romance languages, philosophy, and speech).[27] More moderate and conservative professors are from the schools of engineering, business management, and even education and journalism. This has been reflected down the line to both graduate and undergraduate students. However, all such generalizations are only impressionistic and have led to an unnecessary and unbecoming proclivity to stereotype.

---

[27] An interesting exception, especially at the NU Campus, is a small number of radical mathematics professors. In fact, the advisors to SDS at NU have come from two sources: the Sociology Department and the Mathematics Department.

With the rise of student activism, especially the war in Vietnam, pollution, ecology, population growth, and war-related research, many on the so-called "conservative" side, especially among the physical and natural scientists, have "swung to the left"—essentially not to the left but to liberal positions clothed in activist stances. Subsequently, the shift has also filtered down to the students in these schools, (or was the influence in reverse?) Yet whatever changes are taking place, one can venture some tentative generalizations about the NU faculty and to the faculty of other schools.

Faculty members generally are not radicals; they're not flag-waving conservatives either. They are predominately liberals. They fear the left as well as the right. Mark Rudd and Joe McCarthy are synonymous to them. They are, however, according to Hartnett (1969:51), more liberal than the trustees "above" them in terms of party affiliation and ideology and attitudes about higher education. Like their students, faculty members are not apathetic either; that is too simplistic a term. They can simply be described as *non-involved*; they may find activism "interesting," but they are not interested in activist participation. They "do their own thing"—to teach, to contemplate, to do research, to publish, and to reap the professional rewards they have long striven for.

As one radical professor (an advisor to SDS) put it: "The faculty role, to put it bluntly, is to ignore student protest, hoping that it will go away—they view such change as a threat to their status-quo, and in fact, there's little difference between the tenured and untenured professors."

Yet such indifference can readily change to either resistence or support of social change, depending on many factors— the type of school, the influence of the moral thrust of the protest, and/or organized vocal support of such protest. For example, credit for ROTC after a year of SDS protest was finally taken away by *one* school—the College of Arts and Sciences (sometimes referred to as CAS), yet the Technological Institute (referred to as Tech), the Schools of Music, Management (Business), Journalism, and Speech did not do so. Was this an example of the "liberalism" of the CAS faculty? Do the old sterotypes mentioned earlier still work? Again, more research on faculty structure and process is needed before one can answer these questions fruitfully. One thing must be remembered—faculty members have enormous powers over academic concerns and over students, yet little power over non-academic areas (especially outside the university) [28] and over technocratic administrators, (*unless* they wish to confront these issues in a unified maner.)

One general statement about faculty is their general timidity and abhorrence of the violent and the non-intellectual. They decry the lack of civility of many student protesters. They, like most citizens, cannot handle the concept of "violence" and moreover, the indignity they are exposed to by student protesters. For example, Becker (1970:8-11), gives an example of this when he describes how student radicals at a sit-in in 1968 at Stanford University invited faculty members into the occupied building to discuss things with them. But when the faculty members entered, students addressed them, no doubt with some trepidation, by their first names. Whereupon many of the faculty, unable to bear that indignity, left without any discussion with the students.

The point here is that student demands point a threat to faculty status. Becker is quoted:

> "All these people (faculty) have been called by their first names before . . . but of course they react not to the immediate event but to what it symbolizes. It symbolizes . . . students' intention to overturn the existing hierarchy of academic life, a hierarchy that distributes quite unequally participants' power over one another." (1970:9)

Even if it is not to "overturn" but to *equalize* status, this too will be seen as a threat. What next? Take away grades? If you do that—by taking away the "weapon" of compliance: grades—what authority does the teacher have? Possibly, intellect and learning, but these concerns do not crop up in the

---

[28] This view may be attacked by some professors, but it is felt by this author that in the technocratic society, academic intellectuals supply needed answers and raise policy questions, but have little decision-making power on a national level.

answers. The fears remain and the dilemmas of the teacher are still unsolved. Before moving on to the description of students and their life styles, it would be best to describe the decision-making structure of the faculty.

From Diagram 3, one sees this organizational structure. On top, the most powerful voice of the faculty of the entire university is the Faculty Senate. The Senate meets once a quarter (three times a year),[29] and is composed of the chancellor and president of the university; the provost and dean of faculties; the deans of the schools; the chairmen or acting chairmen of the departments of each school; all faculty members with the rank of professor, associate professor, and all assistant professors with five years of service in that rank; other faculty members nominated by their faculties and elected by the senate; the University Librarian; the Registrar; the Director of Athletics; and members of standing committees elected by the senate. All meetings are chaired by the chancellor.

Those excluded from participation on the senate are first-term assistant professors, instructors, research assistants, students, student government leaders, staff, workers, and all outside observers. Even members of the school press (until recently) were also excluded. It is a côterie of the elite faculty on campus and it is a major decision-maker on the larger issues. Because it is large and cumbersome, most policies are hammered out at the committee level or are made at the next lower levels—the individual schools and the departments in those schools. The senate considers matters of general interest to the university and legislates on those affecting the interests of more than one school. It may make recommendations to the provost for referral to the chancellor and the president and through them to the board of trustees, or to any faculty, on matters of general educational policy. There are also a few major committees of the senate.

---

[29] During emergencies, such as the Kent State strike or the Black students' "take-over" of a university building in 1968, the Senate can meet more often.

Diagram 3
Faculty Organization

University Senate

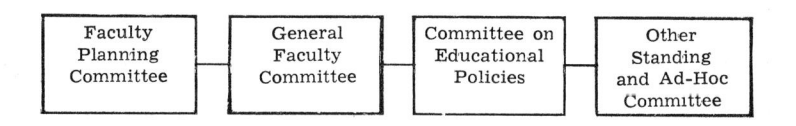

| Faculty Planning Committee | General Faculty Committee | Committee on Educational Policies | Other Standing and Ad-Hoc Committee |

Deans of Schools and Colleges

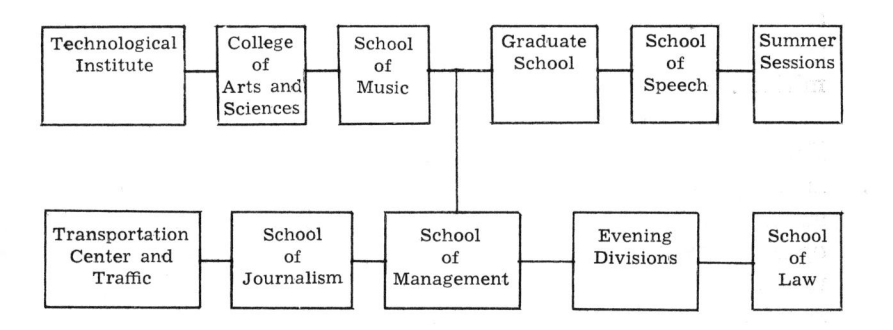

| Technological Institute | College of Arts and Sciences | School of Music | Graduate School | School of Speech | Summer Sessions |

| Transportation Center and Traffic | School of Journalism | School of Management | Evening Divisions | School of Law |

Faculty Members

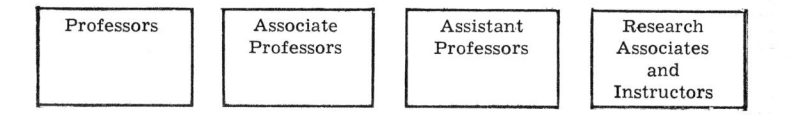

| Professors | Associate Professors | Assistant Professors | Research Associates and Instructors |

General Faculty Committee (GFC): The GFC is one of the most influential bodies in the university. It is a fifteen-man (no women) standing committee of the senate composed of elected representatives from each school of the university with a rotating membership and chairman. This committee provides liaison between members of the several faculties and the administrative officers and acts on university issues either referred to it by the faculty and administration or initiated for consideration by its own members. It is an important committee since it will be referred to later over the issue of ROTC protest.

Committee on Educational Policies (CEP): A second major senate committee is the CEP which functions as a coordinate faculty agency with the GFC, the chairman of which is ex-officio a member. Appointed by the chancellor from recommendations made after consultation with the GFC, the ten-man (no women) CEP is responsible for advising administration and faculties on long-range educational issues and for directing activities of a number of other university faculty committees.

Faculty Planning Committee: This committee's major function is to provide information for the university's long-range educational programs. Its well known report *A Community of Scholars* was a two part comprehensive analysis of the undergraduate curriculum, his student life outside the classroom, interdisciplinary educational programs, and a review of instructional resources and classroom space. All are necessary in the long-range plans of a university.

These are the three major senate committees. One other should be added—the *Committee on Naval Science,* a special one formed in March 1970 to administer the Naval Reserve Officers Training Corp (usually referred to an NROTC) when it formally leaves the CAS in the spring of 1971. This special committee arose as a response to the student protest of NROTC's presence on campus. The role of the Faculty Senate (particularly the GFC) and the role of the CAS vis-à-vis the status of NROTC will be discussed in a future chapter.

Let us conclude this section with an analysis of decision-making. The prime function of the Faculty Senate is to efficiently and harmoniously handle the larger faculty issues of the university and to plan and carry through both long and short-range educational policies. When this dovetails with the views of the administrators and the board of trustees, and it usually does, then there is a minimal amount of problems, almost none. However, when there is conflict over such decision-making, then there is a struggle and in most instances, the administration acquieses and accepts the Faculty Senate decision. But whatever the conflict, it is usually shrouded in secrecy to most students and to the general public. As one administrator put it: "We don't like to display our dirty laundry."

For example, there was a struggle during the last few years over deferred rush (the timing of fraternity and sorority membership drives). In this case, the decision of the Faculty Senate in favor of deferred rush went against the feelings of the trustees and most of the administration. On the issue of ROTC, as will be shown, there was strong trustee and administrative support and any anti-ROTC decision was seen as a "loss" to the administration. In this case, the Faculty Senate compromised by keeping ROTC on campus yet altering its academic credentials by questioning the academic quality of the program. And finally, on the issue of the Kent State strike, the faculty and administration (with some dissent from trustees and a few alumni) concurred that it would be apropos to close down the school. What makes prediction difficult is that not all issues are handled in the same way; each really is struggled with separately.

The question of precedence, so common in legal institutions, is not always considered in academia to be an overriding consideration especially when extenuating circumstances, political pressure, or economic concerns enter the picture. Each conflict, each series of student protest essentially do three things: they lay the groundwork for further protest, they upset and/or realign the supporting sectors of the university, and they "test" the power and influence of the administration and faculty. Before describing over which areas they do have power and/or influence, let us define these terms. To some sociologists, these two concepts are closely related but not identical, since power (or prestige or position in a hierarchy may contribute to the potential for inter-personal influence, but does not determine the extent to which influence actually occurs. (See Merton, 1949: 217 and *passim*.) On the other hand, H. D. Lasswell states that power and influence are synonymous: "The study of politics is the study of influence and the influential." (1936:3) However, it seems safe to say that though the two are often highly correlated, they do differ in the following way. Influence, rather than power, is noted where the change in behavior of the influenced is due to advice, manipulation, imitation, or the like instead of coercion or the exercise of formal authority. Thus influence can be defined as any changes in behavior or a person or group based upon advice, manipulation, or informal control. Power, on the other hand, is the ability (exercised or not) to produce a certain occurrence through a more demanding, more formal, and more legal exercise connected with a formal authority. (See Ehrmann, 1964: 332-333 for more on this.) Though the distinction is often blurred, it does seem that university decision-making is based more on influence, than on power. This is in line with the perception of the university as a somewhat closed community and one that wishes to reach decisions not through formal power plays, but through the informal means. This seems to be the case of the faculty-administration relationship. However, when students "barge in" and demand access to this power and influence, they are usually dealt with in a more formal coercive way, though informal manipulation is also present to a great degree. Plus, there is the tenacity with which faculty and administration hold on to existing power arrangements and see student intrusion as upsetting the careful sharing of power and division of labor that the two have built over the years. It is this tenacity, as Becker (1970:8) points out, which has "convinced students that they have no chance of ever winning anything worth winning under present circumstances." Let us now describe the areas of such power and/or influence.

The following diagram as seen from the *administration point of view* is important:

Diagram 4

University Influence and Decision-making

	Influence	Little Influence
Decision Making Power	A	NULL
No Decision Making Power	B	C

Now what are these areas? In position A, are the following topics where the trustees, chancellor and some vice-presidents have a fair amount of unchecked power, where they don't need or even seek faculty and students' opinions. Here they hold both power and influence.

1. University expansion
2. Stock portfolio
3. Tuition
4. Budgetary concerns
5. Building programs

In areas where they are powerful influences but have no decision making powers, the following are included in position B.

1. Curriculum
2. Credit for courses
3. Promotions
4. Deferred rush
5. Parietal hours

And finally in position C, where they have little influence and no decision making powers, the following are all under student control:

1. Student carnivals
2. Student government elections
3. Student publications
4. All minor student activities

One then can see in bold face from this diagram what little power students have and over what minor areas they have any influence. Faculty has much more power over its areas but can be highly influenced by administrators and trustee members. But the major point to be made is that most student protest demands though addressed to the administration, could be more favorably addressed to the faculty directly, though this is rarely done because it is the administration that is seen as "all-powerful" and is viewed as the "enemy"—not the faculty. These points will have important consequences later when such complex issues as NROTC or Black student demands are the foci of student protest. Here both the faculty and the administration have decision-making powers. Parts of the conflict can be resolved by one body and parts by the other. Much of this depends upon how the question is perceived and understood (or misunderstood). For example, the issue of ROTC (or war related stock and biological-chemical warfare research) is seen by student protesters as a *political* question, not an academic one. Yet, the faculty and the administration respond to it in academic terms. To answer the students' demands otherwise would be to legitimate the correctness of their political perspective, and this the administration does not want to do. The same is true in the case of drug users. The user may want a medical perspective; his antagonists wish to use a legal or criminological one. Black militants use political tactics and wish to be responded to on political or economic terms; instead, they are usually labeled "criminals" or political subversives and are treated as such. To do otherwise, would be again to legitimate both the person (or group) and his claims. This gap between what is asked and what is given, and how the entire issue is perceived and then acted upon, is the core of what defines protest and can lead to seemingly zero-sum confrontations—what one side gains, the other side loses. Differing definitions of the situation can lead to such conflict.

REFERENCES

American Association of University Professors Bulletin, "On the Financial Prospects for Higher Education." 54 (June): 182-205, 1968.

Beck, Hubert P. *Men Who Control Our Universities.* New York: Kings Crown Press, 1947.

Becker, Howard S. (ed.) *Campus Power Struggle.* Chicago: Aldine. 1970.

Cartter, Alan. *An Assessment of Quality in Graduate Education.* Washington, D.C.: American Council of Education, 1966.

Daily Northwestern. "Know Your Board of Trustees." (October 31): 11-20, 1969.

Domhoff, G. William. *Who Rules America?* Englewood Cliffs, N.J.: Prentice-Hall, 1967.

Ehrmann, Henry W. "Influence." Pp. 332-333 in Julius Gould and William L. Kolb (eds.), *A Dictionary of the Social Sciences.* New York: The Free Press, 1964.

Hartnett, Rodney T. *College and University Trustees: Their Backgrounds, Roles, and Educational Attitudes.* Princeton, N.J.: Educational Testing Service, 1969.

Kelman, Herbert C. *A Time to Speak: On Human Values and Social Research.* San Francisco: Jossey-Bass, 1968.

Lasswell, H. D. *Politics, Who Gets What, When, How.* New York: McGraw-Hill, 1936.

Merton, Robert K. "Patterns of Influence." Pp. 180-219 in Paul F. Lazarsfeld and Frank Stanton (eds.), *Communications Research, 1948-49.* New York: Harper and Brothers, 1949.

Mills, C. Wright. *The Power Elite.* New York: Oxford, 1956.

Northwestern University. *Northwestern University, Facts—1969.* Evanston, Illinois, 1969.

Rauh, Morton A. *The Trusteeship of Colleges and Universities.* New York: McGraw-Hill, 1970.

Ridgeway, James. *The Closed Corporation.* New York: Random House, 1968.

Sklar, Bernard. Faculty Culture and Community Conflict: An Historical, Political, and Sociological Analysis of the October 18, 1967 Dow Demonstration at the University of Wisconsin. Unpublished Dissertation (abstract). University of Chicago, 1970.

U.S. Office of Education. *Earned Degrees Conferred—1967-68.* Washington, D.C.: U.S. Office of Education, 1968.

Chapter II
The History of Political Activism At Northwestern

In writing the history of political activism on the campuses of the United States, one comes to the dilemma of assigning that event which "touched it all off." This is difficult. There are important landmarks, but to *precisely* define which single circumstance signaled the "age of protest" is to badly interpret history. It is not one event, but a series of them, a process within the social movements of the 1960's that thrust political activity into the midst of academia.

Students as a political force arose in the 1960's to fill a vacuum that the so-called Silent Generation of the 1950's had promoted. And it caught educators, social scientists, and indeed nearly everyone by surprise. The following statements point out how completely unaware most observers were of the cataclysm to come. In 1957, one writer deplored the "dull conformity" among students and lamented that "the day of student action, of petitions, eager discussions and picket lines is long gone," (Shapiro, 1957:212). In 1959, Louis E. Reik suggested that "students . . . have too much to lose to run the risk of open rebellion during their college days," (1959:451), while Clark Kerr noted that "employers will love this generation, they are not going to press many grievances. . . . They are going to be easy to handle. There aren't going to be any riots."

Meanwhile the college population in other parts of the world was deeply involved in politics. In fact in the 1950's when one talked about student activism, it was usually in some "far-off" country like Spain or Japan. Latin American students, following a long tradition of political activism, played significant roles in bringing down such dictators as Peron of Argentina in 1955 and Perez Jimenez in Venezuela of 1958. Students were prominent in the abortive uprisings against the Communist regimes in Hungary, Poland, and East Germany. In 1960, Japanese students brought down the government with their massive riots against the Security Treaty with the U.S., and students had a considerable part in overthrowing the dictatorship of Rhee (Korea) and Mendes (Turkey). Students, as a political force to be reckoned with, were becoming an international "problem," but American students were still quiescent. One frustrated activist complained that:

> ... to attain self-discovery, we must dissent, disaffiliate ourselves from all the cliched and stereotyped burdens the educated and the non-educated would impose; dissent from the dogma of the politician, the business man, the critic, and the truck driver. If our "revolt" seems mild, it is because we have not found anything to promote. ... (Kunitz, 1957:201)

In 1960, Northwestern was still greatly involved with football games, homecoming queens, and fraternity hazing. Student activism didn't exist, almost. Two Northwestern professors and a student in 1960 participated in a peace and disarmament march through the city, and in a mock political election between Kennedy and Nixon, the latter received 62 percent of the vote. Eight years later, Nixon was to lose the mock election and Eugene McCarthy was to be nominated, the first Democrat to be so chosen in the history of Northwestern. NU was to change drastically, along with the rest of the nation, during these years.

In 1960, the vacuum was suddenly filled. On February 1, four Black students from North Carolina Agricultural and Technical College sat in at a segregated lunch counter in Greensboro, and were arrested for trespassing. Within a month, their lead had been followed by students from predominantly Black colleges and high schools in the South; the sit-in, accompanied by marches, picketing, and boycotts of various kinds, became the characteristic tactic of the new movement for integration. At NU's mock political convention in 1960, a plank in the convention platform included "an expression of sympathy for Negro college students in the South while not necessarily sanctioning their tactics of civil disobedience." The struggle for civil rights became the first focus of activism in the sixties. Later the issues would shift to the war in Vietnam, ROTC, and pollution. The voices would get angrier; the tactics more violent.

During the early sixties, campus conservatism also enjoyed a brief boom. The Young Americans for Freedom (YAF) achieved some initial successes and the candidacy of Barry Goldwater later brought temporary strength and fleeting encouragement to the ranks. However, David Riesman could remark in 1963 that "campus conservatives must now be much more vocal and better organized to expound their views because they are increasingly in a minority." (McNeely, 1963:128). Lipset and Altbach (Lipset, 1967:207) have concluded that:

> The conservative student organizations, despite their impressive financial and organizational backing, have not been notably successful in building a movement which has much commitment from its membership, nor have they made any real impact on the campus.

In fact, in the early sixties, especially over the issues of free speech such as at Berkeley in 1964, some conservative groups joined the radical protesters, but by the late 1960's, YAF was offering a different appeal, as a rallying-point for the anti-protester. As for the middle liberal segment of students, one could still speak of "classroom sobriety" and the "serious intellectual interests" of students in the early sixties. In fact, one can still speak in similar tones now in the early seventies. Though it is no longer possible to speak of a silent generation, it is still a fact that the student activists, while conspicuous, were and still are a small proportion of the total population, and on some campuses, are barely in evidence. Yet still in all, in the span of a decade, American students had become in Richard Flack's words, a young intelligentsia in revolt.

Yet NU was still fairly quiet. Activism on a noticeable scale did not begin until the fall of 1965. Yet in the five years leading up to this date, the following events occurred that set the foundation for Northwestern's entrance into student radicalism:[1]

May 1960: Sixty-eight students were arrested in a protest demonstration organized against the House Un-American Activities Committee (HUAC) which was meeting in San Francisco to investigate presumed subversive activity. It is possible that this was the first event that was the catalyst for the New Left, and not Berkeley which began over four years later.

November 1960: John F. Kennedy was elected president.

March 1961: The Peace Corps was organized under the Kennedy administration's initiative.

Summer 1961: SNCC, the Student Non-violent Coordinating Committee, began its Black voter-registration campaign in McComb, Mississippi.

June 1962: After several months of preparation, the manifesto of the Students for a Democratic Society (SDS), the Port Huron Statement, was approved. SDS was founded and soon chapters appeared on campuses.

October 1962: For the first time, a Black man, James Meredith, was admitted to the University of Mississippi. Violence followed.

October 1962: The Cuban missile crisis occurred.

November 1962: Several peace candidates, including Professor H. Stuart Hughes of Massachussetts, ran for election

---

[1] For a complete history, chronologically, of the New Left activity, see Teodori (1969). For a more concise statement, see Obear (1970). For an earlier historical account, now somewhat dated, see Newfield (1966). For a fine documented report, see Jacobs and Landau (1966). For an analysis of the Berkeley "turning point," see Draper (1965), Lipset and Wolin (1965), and Miller and Gilmore (1965). For the most comprehensive bibliography on not only the history, but the sociological and psychological roots, of student activism, see the excellent reader compiled by Foster and Long (1970); see especially Foster (1970: 27-58).

outside the two traditional parties. Young movement activists became involved in the campaigns. Eight years later, this was to occur again with the impetus of the Movement for a New Congress; six years later, it was to be the youthful followers of the McCarthy-McGovern-Kennedy campaigns.

Winter 1963: Michael Harrington's *The Other America* was published, and revealed to the public the extent of poverty in the U.S.A.

April 1963: Dr. Timothy Leary, who was to become a "guru" to the future counter-culture, and Professor Richard Alpert were dismissed from Harvard for experimenting with LSD on students.

August 1963: The now-famous civil-rights march on Washington took place. Over 200,000 attended.

November 1963: John F. Kennedy was assassinated in Dallas. The era of "Camelot" was over.

March 1964: Malcolm X broke with the Black Muslims and proposed a plan for an all-Black nationalist party.

April 1964: The Progressive Labor Party (PLP), a pro-Peking group, emerged from a split in the Communist party. Five years later it was to split from SDS, away from the Weathermen faction, and away from the Revolutionary Youth Movement II. While it was always separate organizationally, it helped SDS develop a class-consciousness and an explicitly anti-imperialistic orientation that SDS had not articulated previously. For further discussion, see *Debate Within SDS* (Radical Education Project: 1969).

Summer 1964: A large civil rights project mobilized in the South. The goals were voter registration, freedom schools, and the organization of local communities. Several Blacks and whites were killed.

Summer 1964: Harlem erupts in riot.

August 1964: The Mississippi Freedom Democratic party delegation was not accredited at the Democratic Party convention. This event led to a disillusionment of both Blacks and whites with "working in the system."

September 1964: Political activity, specifically table-manning by "off-campus" groups was prohibited at the University of California at Berkeley, thereby touching off the first, wide-scale student protest of the sixties.

October 1964: The Free Speech Movement (FSM) was founded at Berkeley.

November 1964: Lyndon B. Johnson was elected president.

December 1964: More than eight hundred students were arrested at Berkeley during an administration building sit-in; teaching assistants strike; university paralyzed for several days; U of C President Clark Kerr agrees to FSM demands; nationwide publicity, Free Speech Movements founded at other universities. The FSM was spearheaded *not* by SDS as is commonly believed, but by an amalgamation of both pro-civil rights and PLP groups.

February 1965: Malcolm X was assassinated in New York

February 1965: The systematic American bombardment of North Vietnam began.

March 1965: Martin Luther King leads march from Selma to Montgomery, Alabama, as a means of applying pressure for new Voting Rights Bill in Congress. There was violence, and Viola Liuzzo, a white activist from Detroit, is killed.

March 1965: The first teach-in on the war in Vietnam was held at the University of Michigan. Teach-ins are held at hundreds of colleges; Northwestern is not among them.

March 1965: SDS sponsors a 25,000 man march on Washington to protest the Vietnam war. The reputation of SDS grows on a national level, and within three months, the number of local chapters increases from 35 to more than 100.

March 1965: This busy month ends with American troops invading the Dominican Republic in order "to prevent a Communist take-over."

June 1965: Julian Bond, one of the leaders of SNCC, is elected to the Georgia state legislature, but is refused a seat because of his anti-war stand.

August 1965: With the signing of the new civil rights law, the phase of legal struggle in the South comes to an end. The first all-Black party, the Lowndes County Freedom Organization, is formed in Alabama.

Summer 1965: The Black ghetto of Watts erupts in revolt in Los Angeles. Martin Luther King states that the civil rights movement was insufficient to deal with the problems of Black people. The Black liberation movement changes gears here. The action begins to shift from the South to the North and West; from the rural areas to the urban; from integration to liberation and "Black Power."

Summer 1965: One of the first Free universities founded in New York; more than twenty courses (that ranged from politics to sex) attract over 200 students.

Summer 1965: Following the first burning of draft cards by students and young non-students, Congress approves a law making such acts punishable as crimes.

October 1965: Nationwide anti-war demonstrations sweep the nation. While Norman Morrison, a Quaker pacifist, immolates himself in front of the Pentagon to protest the Vietnam war, Northwestern University begins to join the rest of the nation with the formation of an SDS chapter. It is a year after the FSM movement began, and three years after SDS was founded at Port Huron, Michigan.

SDS at NU merged with a local civil rights group called FREE, For Real Estate Equality, and a student group called Students for Liberal Action. Its first meeting during October of 1965 drew a polyglot group of 80 people, graduate and undergraduate students, Greek and non-Greek. In fact, SDS was founded by two ex-sorority girls; its first faculty chairman was a young sociology professor. Its first event occurred during Halloween of 1965—an anti-war demonstration.

It is interesting to note that at first the NU administration was quite *happy* to have an SDS group on campus; it helped to change the image of the school from a nineteenth century "country club" to a twentieth century "with-it" kind of university. In fact it is important to note that in the early days of student activism such activity was welcomed and not considered threatening as it is today. Obear (1970:17) makes the point quite clear:

> To many faculty and administrators, the new activism was entirely admirable, even if it was an occasional source of embarrassment when dealing with conservative donors or trustees. Protest was aimed at integration, an ideal close to the hearts of Northern academic liberals, and to a lesser extent at peace, a barely less acceptable goal.

This warm welcome was soon to wear out. As the "heroic" civil rights period, 1960 (or possibly 1955) to 1964, drew to a close, and as Black militants moved the focus of action to the North, so too did white militants move the focus from the area of Black rights to student rights. Students began to turn to the campuses themselves. As early as 1963, Clark Kerr could observe in his Godkin Lectures that

> ... students are restless. ... There is an incipient revolt against the faculty; the revolt that used to be against the faculty *in loco parentis* is now against the faculty *in absentia*. The students find themselves under a blanket of impersonal rules for admissions, for scholarships, for examinations, for degrees. It is interesting to watch how a faculty intent on few rules for itself can fashion such a plethora of them for the students. The students also want to be treated as distinct individuals. (1963:103).

It was during these same lectures that Kerr coined the term "multiversity," and it was Kerr's protagonist at Berkeley, Mario Savio, who was a year later to refer to the multiversity as a "knowledge factory." The university began to be seen as a technocratic institution, a "machine" Savio said, "so odious, you've got to make it stop." Due to the post World War II "baby boom" and because of an expanded economy, increased population growth, and enlarged educational goals America found itself with a large, restless, and relatively privileged class of students. The effect of this outgrowth began about 1962-64 (coincidentally with the formation of SDS in 1962 and the Berkeley revolt in 1964). Yet it was a class or sub-culture, if you will, that held little power over the decisions that affected its own life. This imbalance between privilege and power; this gap between childhood and adulthood; this situation set up reverberations that diffused and spread from

Berkeley to many campuses across the country. Northwestern was still in 1966 at an early level of student activism; the issues of men's visitation and curfew hours were in the forefront. As Stokely Carmichael was explaining Black Power to the American public in the summer 1966, NU, under student protest, was reexamining its admissions policies in order to admit a more diverse student body. Future admissions included more Blacks, more Easterners, more Jews, and more "hip" types. All these policies had an unanticipated effect—these new people were to be in the vanguard of student protest on the campus. This was true for campuses across the country. New admission policies brought not only a diversified student body, but a more militant one. Though it is true that other considerations besides these policies "caused" the student unrest, it is equally true that administrators would have probably liked to have retracted some of the radical students they admitted in the first place.

The turning point of political activism at NU occurred in April 1967, when its first Vietnam Teach-in was held. It was the biggest event of the school year, attracting over 2,000 people and raising some 500 dollars. It was sponsored by SDS, and many faculty members gave support. Later that spring, the student body at NU was involved in student government elections. One student, Ellis Pines, ran on a Student Power program and led a series of "bitch-ins" which focused student dissent against the administration. He was elected president, and then was thrown out of office because of a grade controversy.[2] For the first time, the administration and some alumni appeared hostile to the student power idea, mild as they were for the time. The issues were still self-determination (over curfew hours) for living units and visitation of males in female quarters.[3] Another issue that was a bit more "militant"

---

[2] Pines was placed on probation for not adequately completing a course, and the rules stated that a student body president could not hold office if he or she were on probation.

[3] Female visitation in male sleeping quarters were widespread and usually discreet. The "double standard" for females was evident.

was for open occupancy. Student pressure caused NU administrators to state their advocacy for open housing laws (for Blacks, Chinese, Mexicans, etc.) in Evanston. The administration said, however, that it was impossible for the university to take an official stand on the issue as an institution.[4] The years 1967 and especially 1968 were among the most tumultuous in recent history. Since the events that occur at one school, such as NU, do not happen in a vacuum, it is best to note the national events that led up to the flowering of political action in the spring of 1967 at Northwestern.

Winter 1967: Demonstrations were held at Berkeley against Marine recruiting, the CIA, and Dow Chemical Company, a maker of napalm. Strikes and arrests followed.

April 1967: A group within the antidraft movement, the Resistance, was formed in California and spread east. After the Northwestern Teach-in on April 13, 1967, a Green Beret, Gary Rader, met with NU SDS to form a Chicago area draft resistance cadre. Rader made national headlines later when he burned his draft card in protest.

April 1967: Many anti-war demonstrations were organized by the Spring Mobilization Against the War. The demonstrations culminated in marches in New York (200,000 people) and San Francisco (65,000 participants). A group of several hundred young men burned their draft cards in New York's Central Park.[5]

The summer of 1967 produced a climate of unrest and fear that set the mood for campus events in the fall: the Israeli-Arab Six-Day War in June; the riots in Newark, Detroit, and other Northern cities; the Vietnam Summer project where over 30,000 student volunteers in more than 700 cities participated

---

[4] The university, like others such as Columbia in New York, owned land in or near a Black neighborhood. University expansion to meet increased student body needs has become another issue for campus activists, including those at NU.

[5] For an excellent visual reference, see the movie *Far From Vietnam* directed by Jean Luc-Godard, Alain Resnais, Chris Marker, and others.

in leafletting, meetings, and other events. Northwestern students participated in the latter. The fall quarter opened with some trepidation and much anticipated excitement as fall sessions have opened in many schools every year since, with both students, faculty, and administration never quite knowing what to expect.

Just before school opened, two events occurred whose causal implications are still debated. The National Conference for New Politics met in Chicago and the national Black Power conference met in Newark. The New Politics conference was the first, last, and largest meeting of liberals and radicals, both Black and white, ever held up to that time.[6] The conferences' short-range effect on the local campuses was undetectable; its long-range impact was decisive. Black and white radicals broke away to develop ideology and tactics independently, being somewhat reconciled later by the Black Panther Party, and especially Eldridge Cleaver and Huey Newton, who saw a place for white radicals in the Black movement. The Black Power conference set the ideological, if not the tactical, foundation for the Black students' sit-in at Northwestern seven months later.[7]

While new students attended an orientation week, SDS at NU set up a "disorientation" week to attract adherents and begin the educational and radicalization process for the year. Again, it must be mentioned that the new university policies recruited more Blacks and more "big city cosmopolitans." This made it possible for larger and more effective radical student "sub-cultures" and orientations to develop in the school. Fraternities and sororities, so long a dominant voice in student

---

[6] For one of the best analyses of this most important, yet nearly ignored conference, see Ridgeway (1967). The conference exemplified not only the failure of grass-roots support for a coalition between Blacks and whites, but between leftist students and liberal trade unionists.

[7] In any historical and sociological analysis of the New Left, and the definitive study has yet to be written, direct causal effects are often counter-productive and often difficult to ascertain. Only a macro-perspective is of value. Influences are better seen as a process, that is both unilinear *and* circular, and always complex.

affairs, were beginning to wane in importance. Attempts were made to adapt: two Black girls were pledged to sororities; Jews were admitted to previously all-Christian fraternities; discriminatory clauses were soon dropped. The rah-rah-pledge-or-die myth lingered on, but the exuberance was fading. Working against the Greeks was a new feeling of pride among Independents (non-affiliated) students. No longer dependent on Greeks for housing and social life, Independents (including of course SDS) were forming their own social and political groups, as well as taking over campus organizations once dominated by Greeks.

Events began to be telescoped in 1968 and a "snowball effect" occurred with event after event being added. But a few events must be mentioned before the new year of 1968 began.

October 1967: The march on the Pentagon, chronicled in Norman Mailer's *Armies of the Night* took place. Soon after, the Yippies were formed, bridging the gap between the hippies, who were making a street corner in San Francisco famous around the world, and the political radicals. A specifically American, "Yankee Dixie-Doodle," type of revolutionary force was being formed.

November 1967: The Peace and Freedom Party, an independent third party, was registering citizens in California.

December 1967: Eugene McCarthy entered the race for the Democratic presidential nomination, enjoying a large youthful following. Northwestern at its mock political convention overwhelmingly chose McCarthy as its nominee. Many NU students and faculty began to work in his campaign.

In February 1968, a demonstration was held against Dow Chemical. Senator McCarthy won initial victories in the primaries that same month. Robert Kennedy then entered the presidential race. Then a series of bracing events occurred that led up to the Black students' sit-in in May 1968.

March 1968: Candidates for the Peace and Freedom— Black Panther party coalition were placed on the ballot in the California primary elections.

March 1968: President Lyndon B. Johnson announced he was not going to run for re-election in the November presidential race. Student activists considered this a victory for the "Movement." Vice-president Hubert Humphrey enters the presidential race.

April 1968: Martin Luther King is assassinated in Memphis by a white man. Following his death, riots occurred in Black ghettoes in Northern and Southern cities, including Washington, D.C. In Oakland, Black Panther members Bobby Hutton is killed by police, and Eldridge Cleaver is wounded and taken prisoner. After King's death, Northwestern officially cancels classes, for the first time in history. A demonstration by more than 300 students on campus brought about an official university commitment to open housing in Evanston—an action that a year ago the school administration did not want to take.

April-May 1968: Columbia University was occupied by Black and white students. The sit-in with its subsequent police "bust," drew national attention and is one part of the historical axis of which Berkeley was the other. The causes of the demonstrations and occupations were the university's expansion into the Harlem community, the close connection between Columbia's research institutes and the CIA, and the administration's policy of close cooperation with the country's large defense and war-related corporation.

May 1968: The student unrest became international in scope with outbreaks in Germany, Italy, and France. The movement, begun by French students in a coalition with worker's unions, threatened the government and may have led to the resignation of President Charles DeGaulle.

While the air was still heavy with tear gas at Morningside Heights and at the Sorbonne, Northwestern witnessed another "turning point"—Black students (120 in all) seized the bursar's office to begin a 38-hour sit-in. The event made national headlines and increased tension between students and administrators. SDS members in a show of support, sat-in at the office of Dean of Students. There were no arrests and no damage to persons or property. Conciliation was worked out peacefully, but the administration, smarting from the publicity and

53

subsequent trustee and alumni criticism for capitulating to the Blacks, vowed never to allow another sit-in or similar protest without punishment. NU, like other schools across the country, began then to take a "harder" line against student protest. The agreement reached with the university called for increased Black enrollment, administration consultations on financial aid and admissions, a statement by the university admitting previous racism, the availability of living quarters for Blacks who want to live together, plus a "Black House" to hold meetings.

Personnel shifts were evident during the year also. The President, Roscoe Miller, was appointed Chancellor and a new post of President was later filled by Robert Strotz, the past Dean of the College of Arts and Sciences. Strotz was appointed, without student consent, in July 1970 after a two year search. The Dean of Faculties, Payson Wild, was named Provost. A new Dean of Students was needed when the previous one, Roland J. Hinz, announced that he would concentrate on another position, Vice-President for Student Affairs. Hinz played a large part in conciliating the Black sit-in and would play a "middleman" role in the ROTC protests that were to follow.

As the university drew near to commencement in June of 1968, the nation was shocked by the assassination of Presidential candidate Robert F. Kennedy immediately after his primary victory in California. The summer at Northwestern was quiet, but the rest of the nation was not as the following events will show:

Summer 1968: Berkeley erupts with demonstrations expressing solidarity with the French revolt.

July 1968: Cleveland was the scene of four days of violent confrontation, with eight Blacks and three policemen killed. There were fewer summer riots, but there was a tendency for more militant organization by Blacks.

August 1968: Troops from the U.S.S.R. and other Warsaw Pact nations invade Czechoslovakia.

August 1968: One of the major events in the history of the New Left and America took place in Chicago before TV viewers. Under a state of siege and with police and the National Guard patroling the streets, Hubert Humphrey won the Presidential nomination at the Democratic convention. Thousands of people, demonstrators, bystanders, reporters, and even a few delegates, were brutally beaten or tear-gassed. Hundreds were arrested, including Lee Weiner, a Northwestern sociology graduate student and one of the demonstration organizers. The marches were coordinated by the National Mobilization Committee to End the War, the "Yippies" of the Youth International Party, and other New Left and Black Liberation groups.

As school began for NU students in the fall of 1968, a new issue was soon to be focus of student unrest: the question of ROTC. The next chapter will deal more particularly with this issue, especially the decision-making of faculty and administration vis a vis the status of ROTC. Let us conclude with a tongue-in-cheek analysis by the *Daily Northwestern* in a retrospective comment:

> Many contend that more must happen before Northwestern will be truly responsive to the challenges of the 70's. But it is a sobering thought to compare the change NU has undergone in ten years with the millions of years it took an ape to evolve into man. (December 10, 1969:14.)

REFERENCES

Daily Northwestern. "Retrospective: What Difference 10 Years Make." (December 10): 4, 8, 14, 1969.

Draper, Hal. *Berkeley: The New Student Revolt.* New York: Grove, 1965.

Foster, Julian. "Student Protest: What Is Known, What Is Said." Pp. 27-58 in Julian Foster and Durward Long (eds.), *Protest: Student Activism in America.* New York: Morrow, 1970.

Foster, Julian and Durward Long (eds.). *Protest: Student Activism in America.* New York: Morrow, 1970.

Jacobs, Paul and Saul Landau. *The New Radicals: A Report with Documents.* New York: Vintage, 1966.

Kerr, Clark. *The Uses of the University.* New York: Harper and Row, 1963.

Kunitz, Stanley. "The Careful Young Men: Queens College." *The Nation* (March 9): 200-201, 1957.

Lipset, Seymour M. *Student Politics.* New York: Basic Books, 1967.

Lipset, Seymour and Sheldon Wolin (eds.) *The Berkeley Student Revolt: Facts and Interpretations.* New York: Doubleday, 1965.

McNeely, Dave. "A Wide Variety." *The New York Times Magazine* (November 17):125-130, 1963.

Miller, Michael V. and Susan Gilmore. *Revolution at Berkeley.* New York: Dell, 1965.

Newfield, Jack. *A Prophetic Minority.* New York: Signet Books, 1966.

Obear, Frederick W. "Student Activism in the Sixties." Pp. 11-26 in Julian Foster and Durward Long (eds.), *Protest: Student Activism in America.* New York: Morrow, 1970.

Radical Education Project Collective. Debate Within SDS: RYM II vs. Weatherman. Detroit: Radical Education Project, n.d.

Reik, Louis E. "War of the Generations." *The Nation* (May 16): 451-455, 1959.

Ridgeway, James. "Freak-out in Chicago: National Conference on New Politics." *The New Republic* (September 16): 9-12, 1967.

Shapiro, Charles. "The Careful Young Men." *The Nation* (March 9): 211-212, 1957.

Teodori, Massimo (ed.) *The New Left: A Documentary History* Indianapolis: Bobbs-Merrill, 1969.

Chapter III
The History of ROTC Protest, 1968-1970

Spurred on by the nationwide climate of student protest, a group of faculty members pushed for a motion to form a committee to investigate NROTC. In the fall of 1968, the College of Arts and Sciences established the Heflebower Committee to study NROTC and define its role within the college. At about the same time, the General Faculty Committee of the Faculty Senate appointed the Van Ness subcommittee to study the issues of credit for NROTC courses, location within the university, and other considerations. The Heflebower report dealt with the relationship between the CAS and its *own* Department of Naval Science; the Van Ness committee dealt with the relationship between NROTC and the entire university. As GFC chairman, Professor Richard Schwartz stated: "It was the Vietnam War and the general climate of protest that sparked the creation of these committees, *not* the SDS protest."

On May 8, 1969, the anti-ROTC movement at Northwestern manifested itself in the form of a ten-minute demonstration for the benefit of drilling NROTC midshipmen and observers.[1] Although the anti-ROTC movement *among faculty* had been in existence since the fall of 1968, this protest was the apparent beginning of anti-ROTC *student* activism and concomitant punitive response by the university administration. This ten-minute demonstration led to what most students and faculty

---

[1] Billed as "guerrilla theater," this first example of student protest ended when rain forced cancellation of the NROTC drill.

dubbed an "over-reaction" on the part of the university: of the five SDS students charged with misconduct, one was acquitted, three were found guilty of misconduct, and placed on disciplinary probation, and the last was found guilty of misconduct and suspended for 15 months—the longest suspension in the history of the school.[2] These decisions led to increased anti-ROTC protest; two weeks after the May 8th events, over 600 students, the largest protest demonstration in NU's history, sent NROTC cadets scurrying from two classes, one an indoor marching drill. The NROTC commander quipped:

> Drills used to be so dull . . . this is a classical Freudian transference of feelings of the UDC action to the (NROTC) unit.

Many students and faculty (more than 30 faculty members participated) were incensed over the punitiveness of the disciplinary decisions, as much as over the actual issue of NROTC. The spontaneous protest was larger than any that SDS had, or possibly could have, organized. During this same time, specifically on May 26, 1970, the General Faculty Committee of the Faculty Senate, the most powerful and influential of its committees, announced its report. It proposed, in short, that Northwestern should continue to participate in the NROTC program "in order that it may provide our country with naval officers who have been educated in an environment with a broad liberal background."

During the anti-ROTC protest of May 1969, the General Faculty Committee (the GFC), or specifically the ad hoc committee within it, set up hearings and heard faculty members, SDS members, Associated Student Government (ASG) officers, and NROTC midshipmen, revised its report, and it was adopted by the GFC on May 26, 1969. It finally went to the Faculty Senate five months later, October 1969, and after "furious"

---

[2] The decisions were made under a student-faculty disciplinary body called the UDC, the University Discipline Committee, which was scheduled to be replaced by a more egalitarian system of bodies to mediate conflict (See Chapter 7). In any case, the gross inadequacy of the UDC for handling "major disruptions" was proven by this conflict.

debate, it was accepted except for the most controversial section (section three; see appendix), which recommended taking credit away from all NROTC courses. (Only the individual schools within the university have power to give and rescind credit for NROTC courses.) Another section of the report asked that a special committee within the Faculty Senate be appointed to "review and make recommendations on all" NROTC personnel, "regularly review the course offerings of the naval science department and make appropriate suggestions to improve the program," and finally to act as a supervisory committee to oversee the naval science department when it leaves the College of Arts and Sciences in June 1971. There were no further changes or action by the Faculty Senate, except to confirm who would be on this committee (i.e. to consider adding students to sit on the body).[3]

The Faculty Senate is the most powerful recommendatory body in the university. While little of its legislation is binding, the faculty's decisions are usually accepted as university policy by both the University Cabinet—the chancellor, president, provost, and vice-presidents—and the Board of Trustees. As an indication of this influence, the University Cabinet adopted the faculty's legislation (the GFC report minus the section recommending no credit) as university policy soon after it passed the Faculty Senate.

Parallel to the decisions of the Faculty Senate and the GFC were the proposals and reports of the College of Arts and Sciences (the CAS). An ad hoc committee, the Heflebower committee, produced a report on March 27, 1969, which recommended that "the Department of Naval Science should not be a department of the college . . . effective not later than the end of the academic year 1970-71." Previously, this ad hoc committee had published an exhaustive study of the relationship between CAS and NROTC which examined both the history and present arrangements of the program. (For copies of both of these reports, see the appendix.)

---

[3] As of the time this was being written, during September 1970, no further action had been taken.

In the final report, the characteristics of CAS and the Naval Science Department were compared in an effort to show how the NROTC curriculum differed from the normal academic program. There were considerable differences between them namely:

a) NROTC provides professional training, while the CAS was designed for pre-professional training.

b) Unlike other CAS departments, the Naval Science Department receives its funds from non-university sources.

c) The curriculum and personnel (faculty appointments) of the Naval Science Department are determined by "outside" sources (i.e. the Department of Defense).[4]

d) The academic level of NROTC courses and the academic credentials of NROTC officers were also questioned as being below that of other departments in the college.

On May 28, 1969, the CAS approved the report. Also at that meeting, the faculty as a committee of the whole voted decisively to remove credit for all NROTC courses.[5] The issue was then referred to the Curriculum Committee of the CAS. This committee deliberated through the fall of 1969 and debated whether to recommend to the College of Arts and Sciences to take credit away from *all* NROTC courses or from only those that lacked academic "goodness." The CAS eventually on January 29, 1970, voted to remove credit from *all but three courses*, those being Principles of Naval Organization and Management and Navagation and Naval Operations I and II. A motion to remove all credit was defeated by only three votes,

---

[4] NROTC officers who teach Naval Science courses to NROTC cadets are considered members of the faculty of their respective colleges.

[5] It must be stated that there is a ruling in the CAS that motions made at one meeting can be voted on legitimately only at a second meeting. This can cause much delay on any decisions that are made.

69 to 66. The two-year "battle" finally came to a close two weeks after the Kent State events, on May 19, 1970, when the CAS, in a mail ballot decided not to accept as a part of the forty-five courses required for a bachelor's degree any courses offered by the NROTC unit at Northwestern. This action was to take effect with the class entering in the fall, 1970. It passed 162-123 with 95 abstentions.[6] This outcome may not settle matters since the vote can be taken again and the decision versed in the future. What conclusions can one draw from all this? First, there seems to be no *immediate* cause and effect between a *particular* SDS protest and a *particular* faculty decision. The machinery of decision-making that the faculty undertake, whether it be of the faculty as a whole (represented in the Faculty Senate) or a particular college (the CAS, for instance), runs parallel to and lags somewhat behind the protest of students. This machinery moves slowly. It took the Heflebower committee six months to present its report, then came the first wave of student protest in May of 1969; it then took the CAS an entire year (until May of 1970) to finally decide to remove credit; during this year an entire series of campus-wide and nationwide protests occurred. This slowness can be due in part to the fact that the faculty meets only once a quarter and meets more frequently only during a "crisis," such as Kent State. While it is true that protest "speeds up" this process of faculty decision-making, it can be seriously questioned as to what "speeding up" means. It may mean different things to different people. To some faculty and administrators, the process of change is going "too fast"; for protesting students, the process of change moves at a snail's pace and is much "too slow." Time moves all too slowly for

---

[6] The taking away of credit of NROTC courses affected only CAS majors, who make up 56 percent of *all undergraduates* and more to the point, affects 44 percent of all NROTC midshipmen (65 of 148 are CAS majors). Since Technological (Engineering) Institute and other schools such as the School of Journalism, Music, Speech, Education, or Law did not deny credit, they do not affect their own undergraduates who are in NROTC. More specifically, Tech majors make up 36 percent of NROTC "middies," while the other schools mentioned make up 20 percent.

the powerless; all too quickly for those who are powerful. Let us examine these series of events that composed the year-long anti-ROTC "struggle." [7]

May 1, 1969: Both houses of Congress speed up an investigation of campus disorders. Attorney General John Mitchell calls upon educators to use arrests and prosecutions to "end minority tyranny," and the Assistant Attorney General condemns the "new barbarians" on campus.[8]

May 15-20, 1969: Police and National Guardsmen use shotguns and tear gas (dropped from a helicopter during one incident) on demonstrators at Berkeley, California protesting the university's taking over a tract of land that had recently been made into a "people's park." A curfew is imposed. The event garners nationwide publicity. During that very same week, the anti-ROTC protest began at NU with the "guerilla theater." Other schools are "hit" by protest.

May 27, 1969: ASG at Northwestern calls for a strike of classes. The day before, the GFC presented its report.

May 28, 1969: CAS votes to remove the Department of Naval Science from its college.

May 29, 1969: During the Presidential review of Northwestern's ROTC (where ROTC midshipmen are given honors and awards), over 200 demonstrators attempted (unsuccessfully) to disrupt the activities. Evanston police eventually dispersed the crowd. One person was arrested.

June 5, 1969: At Northwestern's commencement exercises, many students wear red arm-bands or peace symbols as symbolic protest. President Nixon bowed out as commence-

---

[7] As in the previous chapter, I will attempt to interweave national and international events with the campus events. The proof of "cause and effect" is left to the reader; it is the process and the movement that is most important in any case.

[8] This chronology of events is a synthesis of many sources: local (Chicago) and national (*New York Times*) newspapers, the campus paper *The Daily Northwestern,* and the annually published almanacs. In particular see *The New York Times Encyclopedia Almanac, 1970* (Kurtz, 1969).

ment speaker because of fear of possible demonstrations and is replaced by a professor of English, Bergen Evans.

The summers between school years are usually thought to be uneventful, but important events do occur.[9] In a general sense, it gives a student, especially an activist student, time to read, to think, and to reevaluate his political consciousness in order to prepare himself better for the "battles" of the fall. It also gives the administration time to prepare programs and personnel in order to cope with and "put down" the confrontations. For example, more campus police are hired; new weapons (such as tear gas) and programs are tested and devised in order to handle emergency situations; new security devices are adapted to cope with theft, drug usage, or bombings. However, there was one specific event that did have a direct effect on the ROTC protest. In June 1969, the national SDS convention was held in Chicago. After much debate and internal schisms, SDS split into several factions: the Weathermen faction,[10] often called adventuristic or "Custeristic"[11] by other SDS groups, is, however, the first guerrilla movement to develop in America since, possibly, the abolitionists led by John Brown or the IWW (Wobblies) at the turn of the century. The Weathermen can be best compared to the FLN of Algeria in the mid and late 1950's or the Tupemaros of Uruguay. The other factions were RYM I and II (Revolutionary Youth Movement I and II) and the Progressive Labor Party. RYM felt that guerilla warfare was premature, and that it was far better to form working relations with oppressed classes—Blacks, Mexicans, and working-class youth. The Progressive Labor Party follows a strict Maoist "line" and is ideologically similar to RYM I and II. The influence of the split on local SDS chapters was not readily apparent since each SDS chapter is autonomous and

---

[9] The summer sessions of any university, along with the winter months are usually the time of minimum radical activity. The most active seasons are fall (especially October and November) and spring (especially April and May).

[10] The term Weatherman comes from a line in a song by Bob Dylan: "You don't have to be a weatherman to know which way the wind is blowing."

[11] The latter term was first used by the Black Panther Party.

independent, but the effect on SDS at NU was important in that later in the year (October through December 1969) Weatherman-style tactics against ROTC were used and individual Weathermen participated in the "trashing" of ROTC buildings. But in general, there were mixed feelings among NU SDSers about Weatherman action. As one SDS leader put it:

> Weathermen proved that they could be effective street fighters, but whether this will prove useful to the revolutionary movement remains to be seen.

The fact that man had landed on the moon during the summer of 1969 (July 20) and that a month later (August 16), nearly half a million people attended the Woodstock Music and Art Fair in Bethel, New York, did little to raise the spirits or morale of students returning to school that fall. From the very opening day of school, a whole new series of events began to take place:

September 27, 1969: Jerry Rubin, one of the founders of the Yippies, and Bobby Seale, the National Chairman of the Black Panther Party, accuse federal marshalls of "kidnapping" them when they were brought to stand trial in Chicago as two of the "Chicago Eight" who are being tried for conspiracy to incite a riot during the 1968 Democratic National Convention. Lee Weiner, a sociology graduate student at Northwestern, is among the eight.

September 29, 1969: SDS at Northwestern set up a booth during "Disorientation" Week in order to recruit new members.

October 9, 1969: Faculty Senate meets and votes to keep ROTC on campus with credit but refers the matter to a special committee for further study. The meeting is protested by a few professors for "sloppy" procedures and for the Chancellor's alleged attempt to manipulate the meeting toward a pro-ROTC and a pro-credit for ROTC stance.

October 9, 1969: The Faculty of Arts and Sciences at Harvard University votes to call for an end to the Vietnam War. It was thought to be the first time that Harvard's faculty had taken a political stand in opposition to government policy.

October 11, 1969: Presidents of five of the eight Ivy League colleges and of 74 other colleges and universities, speaking as individuals, appeal to President Nixon for a "stepped-up timetable for withdrawal of troops from Vietnam."

October 11, 1969: Radical youth, led by the Weathermen, hold a brief but bloody street battle with police in downtown Chicago to protest the war, political repression, and the Conspiracy Trial. Over 100 protesters are arrested. Individual SDS members at Northwestern did not take part; however, a group of Weathermen who were lodging overnight at a church building at Northwestern were "raided" by police and a few were arrested.

October 15, 1969: Millions of Americans join in protesting the war on the first Vietnam Moratorium Day. Over the objections of conservative students, particularly members of YAF, the Northwestern administration condones the cancelling of classes by professors to discuss the issues in a "manner befitting our academic tradition."

October 18, 1969: Vice-President Spiro Agnew makes the sharpest attack thus far by any administration official on the week's Vietnam Moratorium Day in a speech in New Orleans, referring to the leadership of the protesters as an "effete corps of impudent snobs who characterize themselves as intellectuals."

November 6, 1969: SDS at NU continues its anti-ROTC campaign with a protest.

November 10-13, 1969: Government officials continue "attack" protesters; Vice-President Agnew attacks television network news programs as selective and often biased.

November 13, 1969: Four persons, members of the Weathermen SDS faction, are charged by the FBI with eight recent bombings of corporate or government buildings that have been singled out for "neo-imperialist links to the war machine."

November 15, 1969: The largest mass march on Washington ever held, with over a quarter million demonstrators, protests the Vietnam War. Many NU students and faculty attended. Some also engaged in more violent "trashing" at the Justice Department and the South Vietnamese Embassy that evening.

November 17, 1969: SDS at NU presents an "ultimatum" to the administration asking for a phase-out of ROTC by the spring quarter 1970. During this period, SDS will "continue all phases of its anti-ROTC program," and "increase pressure through day-to-day struggle." (For complete transcript see the "Hourglass Ultimatum" in the appendix.)

November 21-22, 1969: SDS leads protest of about 100 people to administrative offices for a "progress report." A few arrests are made for allegedly accosting security police. The next day, thirty-five people visit the home of the Chancellor Roscoe Miller. After sending his maid out to say that he wasn't in, he appears briefly and then slams door. That afternoon, another protest and "war games" guerrilla theater are acted out at the administrative offices.

November 24, 1969: A group of students, independent of SDS, hold a non-disruptive 54-hour sit-in in the corridor outside the ROTC offices. There is no disturbance, damage, or disruption of any regularly scheduled classes or office hours, so no attempts are made to arrest people. Sit-in ends as campus is "deserted" for Thanksgiving holidays.

December 3, 1969: The ROTC offices are damaged; paint is thrown over files and chairs. The class of a political science professor, who allegedly presented a distorted picture of American imperialism is interrupted during last five minutes of class by a group of SDSers. Disciplinary charges are brought against the students in both events.

December 4, 1969: Chicago police murder Fred Hampton, the Illinois Chairman of the Black Panther Party, and another Panther leader in a hail of shogun and pistol fire during a raid on an apartment near the group's headquarters.

December 5, 1969: SDS holds a protest march in sympathy over the killings from the NU campus into downtown Evanston.

Ten people are arrested when an American flag is lowered to half-mast. Some of the arrestees face multiple charges from previous protests and acts of "trashing."

December 9, 1969: The Chancellor rejects the SDS "Hourglass Ultimatum"; at the same time praising a YAF letter supporting ROTC as a "breath of fresh air."

December 10, 1969: The Conspiracy Trial ends. Soon the end of a decade will occur, and as the 1960's comes to an end, a series of fire-bombings shake the Madison campus at the University of Wisconsin. The ROTC building is one of the structures "hit" by the bombing.

January 12, 1970: The new year and the new decade begin with the damage of the quonset hut that houses ROTC classes. Two days later another attempt at damaging the hut ends with the arrest of five people, one a Weatherman who was not a student at NU. The events cause school-wide discussion and most students and faculty are "turned-off" by the "childish and immature" tactics which are "desperate—ultimately ineffective, even detrimental to their (SDS's) cause." [12] Though 71 percent of the students polled were familiar with the "Ultimatum," only 29 percent sympathized with such a general strategy. As Pollock (1970:13) stated: "The audience (of NU's students and faculty) found it easier to judge the actions of the demonstrators and tended to ignore the real issue at stake: NROTC." In short, the tactics and the trials drew too much attention away from the issue of ROTC, and tended to arouse anti-SDS, rather than anti-ROTC, feelings. This seriously hurt the support for SDS on campus.

January 15, 1970: The administration suspends the four students involved in the quonset hut "trashing" without a hearing.

---

[12] Based on student interviews taken immediately after events by the author.

January 23, 1970: The NU campus is attracted to a "new" issue; a nationally publicized teach-out on pollution took place.

January 29, 1970: The CAS removes credit from six of nine ROTC courses.

February 2, 1970: The University Hearings and Appeal Board (known as UHAB) begins to hear the case of the professor's class being interrupted, since it has been defined as a "major disruption." The Student Hearings and Appeals Board (called SHAB), on the other hand, hears the other cases. Protesting students at times feel that at SHAB they can get a fairer trial because they are tried by a jury of their peers.

February 19, 1970: William Kunstler, an attorney of the "Chicago Conspiracy," speaks at NU. A march of 350 students into downtown Evanston ends in the smashing of stores and a few arrests.

April 15, 1970: The student elections for Associated Student Government (ASG) are held. Eva Jefferson is the first Black to win the presidency of the student body. Two referendums were also held: one on the status of ROTC and the other dealing with the Vietnam War.[13]

April 22, 1970: A national Earth Day is sponsored by anti-pollution groups. NU participates.

April 28, 1970: The linguistics building at NU is firebombed and a stink bomb is placed in the ventilation system of the library. The two events are unrelated and are found not to be the work of SDS.

May 4, 1970: A nationwide student strike takes place as a response to the Cambodia invasion by U.S. troops and the killing of four Kent State students by Ohio National Guardsmen. NU becomes a model of non-violent activity for other

---

[13] The ROTC referendum will be analyzed in a later chapter; the outcome of the Vietnam referendum, however, was as follows: 75 percent of the 3,459 students who voted desired an immediate troop pull-out from Vietnam, 25 percent disagreed.

schools as classes are cancelled. The Faculty Senate and the administration give support to the strike.

May 9, 1970: The last anti-ROTC event led by SDS in its year-long protest culminates in a second "trashing" of the ROTC offices. More than 100 people participate; forty-five are arrested. Ultimately, they were tried by SHAB: about half were convicted and received various fines and disciplinary probations, the other half were acquitted.

May 19, 1970: The CAS takes away all credit from ROTC courses.

May 20, 1970: ROTC moves its offices away from the campus to avoid further "confrontation."

May 21, 1970: Northwestern students endorsed by more than a 3-1 margin a proposal which would suspend classes in the fall for two weeks prior to the Congressional election, in order for them to work for the candidates of their choice.

And after the 1969-1970 school year drew to a close, the following events occurred during the summer:

July 3, 1970: The Faculty Senate refused to schedule a pre-election suspension of classes by a 2-1 vote. But the Senate, in a mail ballot distributed to tenured faculty members, agreed to schedule a "moratorium" on papers and exams prior to the elections. The reasons for refusal of the recess were twofold: scheduling problems and a faculty fear of politicizing the university.

July 10, 1970: The Vice-President and Dean of Students, Roland J. Hinz, resigned in order to "get out of the combat zone." The Dean had the extremely strenuous and frustrating duty of acting as mediator between protesting students and upper-echelon administrators. Looking back over his three years on the job, Hinz said, "there are still things to be done but that substantial improvement and reasonable changes" had taken place during his tenure in office.

July 23, 1970: Robert H. Strotz, formerly Dean of the CAS, was selected as Northwestern's new president with heavy faculty endorsement but with some opposition by student government leaders who said the "appointment would cause widespread student unrest in the fall." At a press conference, Strotz said that despite student opposition, "I have no hesitancy about accepting the presidency, because this is where the action is."

In assaying the year-long ROTC program, who are the "victors" and who are the "losers"? Though deprived of academic credit, removed from the College of Arts and Sciences, and moved far from the center of campus, the NROTC nevertheless remains on the university and can still be considered a prime source of controversy in the future. But radical students are tired of the issue and will most likely view the outcome as a "victory" and move on to other areas. As Professor Marvin Shinbrot, past faculty advisor to SDS, stated:

> The Department of Defense may remove ROTC from campus altogether, like at Harvard. Removal of credit is usually a kiss-of-death for ROTC. But the left on campus paid a high price, maybe too high a price in terms of all the arrests for ROTC's removal.

What of the faculty? To most of them, the issue was seen as an academic one. The academic credentials of ROTC courses and teachers will be upgraded, and academic reforms will most likely "liberalize" and strengthen the ROTC program. The administration and the Board of Trustees, though privately unhappy about the CAS decision for credit removal, has accepted, albeit reluctantly, the recommendations of the Faculty Senate and its ROTC supervisory committee. What was shown, however, and will prove in the long run, more important, is that over the past year, the faculty has steadily increased its influence over administrative decisions. No longer can administrators make decisions *in vacuo*; no longer can professors ignore the "outside world." As Jack Z. Sissors, vice-chairman of the GFC, said:

> The new activism of the faculty is primarily due to the younger professors. There used to be reticence to get up and rock the boat. Now the younger faculty members are more concerned with social issues.

The faculty, the "silent power" in most universities, emerged as the most potent pressure group on the campus, far more powerful than the students. For without faculty support, no amount of radical protest could have made any impact in the status of ROTC. It was only faculty decision-making, albeit aroused by student protest, that made it ultimately possible for changes to take place within the university system. If administrators "listen," it is usually because they seem to be "pushed"—first by the students, and then, most importantly, by the faculty.

What of the ROTC midshipmen and officers? They seemed to be the "silent sufferers" throughout the protest. The midshipmen (at least those in CAS) must now take "over-loads" of ROTC courses in addition to their regular electives and are inconvenienced by the new location of the ROTC offices. Yet they will find the ROTC courses less technical and the instructors more capable. As the new commanding officer of NROTC at NU stated:

> We have tried and hopefully succeeded to modify these courses so that they would become more acceptable. The military nature is reduced and maybe this is a good thing . . . the program is definitely more liberal.

However, as Scott (1969:52) has noted: the reduction of military subjects has broadened the gap between preservice training (in ROTC) and actual military job requirements. ROTC graduates entering active duty in combat-branch line units are unable to handle their initial assignments without considerable additional training. Thus, liberalizing ROTC programs can "hurt" the newly-commissioned ROTC officer who must now spend additional weeks or months learning military skills he did not receive while on the campus ROTC program.

In short, there were no clear cut "winners" or "losers" over the issue of ROTC on the Northwestern campus. Whether it will join the over 24 colleges and universities who have phased out or are in the process of phasing out ROTC units (whether they be Army, Navy, or Air Force ROTC) remains to be seen.[14] It will depend no longer on radical students or faculty interests, but on the Department of Defense, in particular the ROTC offices under the Assistant Secretary of Defense for Manpower Affairs.

In just one short year, Northwestern, as well as campuses across the nation, have undergone dramatic shifts in both tactics and political consciousness. Reaction by police, National Guardsmen, and government has also undergone isomorphic shifts. The period of May 1969 to May 1970 has seen the death of one student at Berkeley's "People's Park" and the death of four students at Kent State. The ideological split within SDS in the summer of 1969 has culminated in the bombings across the nation in the summer of 1970. "Guerrilla theater" has shifted to actual underground revolutionary guerrillas; sit-ins have shifted to bank robberies and bombings of military or military-linked institutions on the campus; kidnapping of both government and university officials and assassinations are no

---

[14] These have usually been the prestigious private universities in the East or Midwest, *not* the large state-supported multiversities. Those disbanding their Air Force ROTC units: Harvard, Boston University, Colgate, Butler, Capital, Tufts, Lawrence, Brown, Union Trinity, Occidental, Rochester, and the Illinois Institute of Technology. Those phasing out their Army ROTC units: Harvard, Dartmouth, Boston University, Yale, Princeton, N.Y.U., Brown, and Washington University. The NROTC or Naval ROTC scheduled for disbanding are: Harvard, Dartmouth, Tufts, Columbia, Princeton, Yale, Amherst, and Brown. (Ehrlich, 1970:4) These figures and facts are, of course, subject to change. They do not include the over 25 schools where ROTC curricula reforms are expected or under way (these range from schools as different as the University of Puerto Rico to Stanford to the University of Kentucky); or to the over 50 campuses where ROTC buildings have been attacked, trashed, or destroyed (usually by fire-bombing) in 1969-70. They include N.Y.U. where 12 separate fires have occurred, Hobart, Kent State, the universities of Alabama, Georgia, Virginia, and Tennessee in the South; Brooklyn College, Hobart, SUNY at Buffalo, Harvard, Maryland, and Princeton, among others in the East; the universities of Colorado, Utah, Nevada, Oregon State, San Francisco State, and nearly all the University of California schools, among others in the West; Ohio, Case-Western Reserve, Michigan, Notre Dame, Chicago, DePaul, DePauw, Wisconsin, Washington (St. Louis), Nebraska, Northern Illinois, Southern Illinois, and of course Northwestern in the Midwest. The attack against ROTC holds to no geographic boundaries. (This information was garnered from numerous newspaper clippings and especially Ehrlich, 1970:4.)

longer insane predictions for the future. The changes that have taken place over the past year or two is perfectly summed up by an article that appeared in the campus newspaper (*The Daily Northwestern,* September 22, 1970:6):

> Two years ago, the hottest topic for freshmen was whether or not to spend $19 for the privilege of saying nothing at a number of free meals given by fraternity row.
>
> Now, fraternity row is strangely quiet.
>
> Two years ago, you were adventurous when you snuck a fifth of scotch or a six-pack of beer into your room.
>
> Now, a major new Student Week activity will be finding the local drug pusher to obtain your weekly supply of "grass."
>
> Two years ago, political discussion centered around the presidential race: Humphrey vs. Nixon.
>
> Now, it centers on speculation on which building will go up in smoke.
>
> Two years was a long time ago.
>
> Now, presidents talk of communication and almost everybody is against the war. Even Richard Nixon.
>
> Now, radicals don't talk in public and now even liberals talk of violence as an acceptable tactic.
>
> And now you can't even protest without the fear of being shot dead.
>
> Two years ago, Eugene McCarthy was a hero and so was Nelson Rockefeller. And two years ago, Spiro Agnew was a bumbling, mumbling fool.
>
> Now, McCarthy's almost forgotten, Rockefeller's sold out to the right and Spiro Agnew, still a fool, has gotten a better speech-writer and has become the reincarnation of Joseph McCarthy.
>
> Two years was a long time ago.
>
> Because the bombing over North Vietnam had just stopped and NU's Black students were almost satisfied over the agreement made after their sit-in in May 1968.
>
> Because peace seemed negotiable.
>
> Two years ago, the Chancellor welcomed peaceful protest.

Now, he advises all freshmen who would think about protesting any other way to go to another school.

Two years ago, students wanted representation on university committees.

Now, they still want representation on university committees.

Two years ago, ROTC was a viable alternative to the draft.

Now, those who join ROTC have "sold out."

Two years ago, Vietnamese villages were burning daily.

Now, Vietnamese villages are still burning daily.

Two years ago was a simple time when coed mixers were a big event.

Two years ago, bell-bottoms and sandals were rarely seen.

Now it's practically a uniform.

Two years ago, city Blacks burned down their own ghettos.

Now, they burn down police stations.

Two years ago, we choked on air pollution no one would admit was there.

Now, we're still choking; people are now admitting the air is polluted but still nothing's being done.

And two years ago, the war in Vietnam was raging.

Now, it rages still, unabated and as deadly as ever.

Two years . . . was a long time ago.

REFERENCES

Daily Northwestern. "Orientation—Two Years Later." (September 22): 6, 1970.

Ehrlich, Howard J. "The 1969-1970 Anti-ROTC Offensive." *The Insurgent Sociologist* 1 (August): 4, 1970.

Kurtz, Seymour (ed.) *The New York Times Encyclopedia Almanac —1970.* New York: New York Times, 1969.

Pollock, Michael. "The NROTC Issue: A Study of the Writings and Rhetoric of Student Activists at Northwestern." Northwestern University: Sociology Department. Unpublished paper, 1970.

Scott, Joseph W. "ROTC Retreat" *Trans-action* 6 (September): 47-52, 1969.

Chapter IV

The Northwestern Student Strike

Since the strike was essential to understanding the process of student protest vis a vis NROTC, it would be beneficial to examine it in detail. On April 30, 1970, President Richard M. Nixon announced an incursion of U.S. troops into Cambodia. On May 2, Tom Hayden called for a national student strike in protest of this action. On Monday, May 4, four students at Kent State University were killed by the Ohio National Guard during an anti-ROTC, anti-Cambodia action demonstration. This set off a chain of events which culminated in the first nationwide student strike in the history of America, and of which the Northwestern University strike was one. What had originally been a moderate groundswell concerning only a few schools mushroomed to tremendous proportions to include over 500 colleges and universities of every classification: public and private; Protestant, Catholic, Jewish, and secular; female and co-ed; black, white, and mixed; activist and conservative; in the North, South, East, and West; sweeping radicals, liberals, and moderates; faculty, students, administrators, and staff.

At Northwestern University on the evening of May 4, after the news of Kent State had broken, the Student Mobilization Committee to End the War in Vietnam, the Vietnam Moratorium Committee, and the Associated Student Government (ASG), plus other groups, comprising some 150 people, met to consider possible action. They had learned of other student strikes from TV and radio reports in the Eastern U.S. (Brandeis University had been headquarters for the National on Strike Information Center, but Northwestern became the headquarters on May 8 when Brandeis was plagued by a weak radio transmitter and people jamming their frequency. Information came in by ham radio and phone, and reports went out 24 hours a day to both local and national news media.) At this meeting, it was decided to call a general student meeting for the next day for Tuesday, May 5, to decide upon the strike vote. At this meeting the ad hoc strike committee was formed as a coalition of the above mentioned groups.

The ASG president, Eva Jefferson, appeared that night to become the leader-designate for the entire strike action. Her recognition as leader designate was fostered by the local media as well as by student acclamation. The media also pounced on the fact that she was Black, a woman, and middleclass. The school paper, the *Daily Northwestern*, carried an editorial that day favoring the strike "as a protest *not against* the university which we are supporting, but rather a strike *of* the university by all university members, students, faculty, and administrators by building renewed opposition to the war." (original emphasis) It also included the text of the strike statement of a joint Ivy League editorial outlining the proposed goals of the national protest:

1) An immediate withdrawal of all American forces from Southeast Asia.

2) Passage of a Senate amendment to the Defense Appropriations Bill to deny all aid for our military and political adventures in Southeast Asia.

3) Mobilization of public support for anti-war caendidates in the primary and general elections.

4) Ending of political repression at home, in particular the government's systematic attempts to eliminate the Black Panther party and other political dissidents.

5) A reallocation of American resources from military involvement abroad to domestic problems, in particular the problems of the beleaguered cities.

6) And the building of support for a massive demonstration in Washington on May 9 to bring to the nation's capitol, in unprecedented numbers, our opposition. (*Northwestern Daily*, May 5, 1970:3)

On Tuesday morning the Chancellor and his cabinet met with the General Faculty Committee of the Faculty Senate to convene the Senate during the afternoon. During this meeting it was decided that the entire university should close down for two days with flags at half-mast and that a protest delegation of faculty and students be sent to Washington. Many faculty were appalled that the meeting was turned into a pro-strike meeting. They wanted time to discuss the consequences of closing down the school but the fervor, fears, and enormity of events literally forced them to acquiesce to pro-strike faculty and students. However, University Provost Payson Wild disagreed: "The administration and faculty really felt the depth of feeling across the country. No one was pushed into this feeling. Our major concern was not to divide the campus." That evening, a mass rally took place with over 5,000 (of a student body of nearly 10,000) students and faculty, and a strike vote was taken. By a huge roar of approval, the students agreed to continue the strike at least until Friday, May 8. It was at this mass meeting that the focus of attention shifted somewhat away from national issues (Kent State and Cambodia) to local issues: opening up publicly the school's stock portfolio; liquidating all war-related stocks; going into the surrounding community of Evanston to speak to citizens; taking academic credit away from ROTC; taking away the guns from campus police; and closing the computer center during the strike. The students agreed to all these demands by voice vote. Eventually all these goals were legitimized by the university except the war-related stocks and the gun-toting security police.

A strike headquarters was set up in the university cafeteria-lounge, but as of yet no clear-cut organizational structure had been formed to transform these short-range goals into viable long-range institutions. Many people were doing many different tasks, but all seemed to be running about with little direction or co-ordination. All activity, leafletting, collecting signatures, and running off strike position papers were all ad hoc in nature. Miss Jefferson, by now the acknowledged strike leader, was swamped with requests from students, alumni, parents, and faculty. A leadership cadre was slowly forming but it was still amorphous and unco-ordinated. On

Wednesday, May 6, the university officially closed "to express its grief over the incidents at Kent State . . ." Another mass student meeting was held that afternoon. It was decided to leaflet cars passing down Sheridan Road (a main artery cutting through the university). There were a number of speeches and a symbolic burial of the four Kent State students. Increased support came from the fraternities and sororities and from students of all political persuasions. Strike banners, red flags, and anti-war literature decorated the Greek houses. The only vocal opposition came from the Young Americans for Freedom and its tiny voice was buried beneath the tumult.[1]

During the afternoon rush hour, leafletting along Sheridan Road continued. Soon afterwards, the road was closed by local police. This action incensed the radical students, including SDS members and Yippies, who built a symbolic counter barricade on the road closing off a two block section fronting the campus. Yet there was no confrontation with police. However, a group of moderate students began to argue with the barricaders. This led to a few scuffles, but the barricade did not come down. City officials and police, it was learned later, were not interested in razing the barricades because they wanted to test traffic patterns down side streets!

That evening there was yet another mass rally at which the Northwestern "declaration of independence" was proclaimed and approved by the people attending. Self-congratulatory speeches were given on the strike's effectiveness, announcements were made, and there was the beginning of a pattern continued throughout the strike: a nightly rock band was present and a concert was given. A feeling of euphoria and

---

[1] The only political action that YAF considered using was to have their tuition partially refunded because of missed classes. This tactic was ignored by the university, but other universities have reacted favorably to such demands, and some have even withheld pay from professors for "illegally" cancelling classes. For example, at the University of Missouri during the Kent State strike held there, the university's Board of Curators voted to withhold part of the paychecks of nine faculty members (eight of whom were sociologists, including the sociology department chairman) who suspended classes during the strike.

comradeship was present, and the smell of pot and incense scented the evening air.

After the rally, three students approached Miss Jefferson with an organizational plan. Up to this time there had been no coherent strike organization. She approved the idea and an organizational meeting was set for the next day. That day (Thursday, May 7) in the morning a meeting was held to set up an effective structure. It had been recognized by the strike leaders that such an organization was necessary to carry out the strike's goals effectively. It was also noted that the long-range goals would have to be clarified and communicated to the university community. The first meeting was indecisive so another was planned after the afternoon rally. It was also recognized that the rallies were beginning to become ineffective, that interest was dissipating, and that new tactics were necessary. But no tactical decisions were made. A party atmosphere began to grow stronger as the weekend of May 9-10 grew near.

The second organizational meeting was held. It was less than orderly but the proposal came to fruition. The problem of goals was evident at the meeting both in the long discussion of strike goals and in the organization that was eventually hammered out. The original proposal was for a series of ten interlocking departments centering around a central co-ordinating committee, a goals and program committee, and a tactics committee. This proposal was rejected in favor of a four part committee group comprised of a steering committee, a grass-roots committee, an information committee, and a New University committee. It was passed with the stipulation that it could be expanded to include oauther functions. Other functions were indeed added and there was a proliferation of extraneous committees which were not tied to the main organization, but were recognized by it. The plethora of such committees was enormous; it validates the thesis that Americans lead the world in its number of voluntary associations. Examples of these are as follows: Black Community relations; day care center (for faculty and graduate students); high schools and junior high schools activity; Yippie "Marauders" (challenging campus police to a water pistol fight—winner turns in his guns); and a labor unions contact committee. The list goes on. Some of these groups fell apart as soon as the strike ended; others lasted until the end of the quarter; a few will be around a long time.

The strike finally ended, for all intents and purposes, with a vote by the student body on Wednesday, May 13, to return to classes. The return ended eight days of intense activity which culminated in the establishment of a New University, or Alternative University which was to be geared to peace-related discussion and research. Approximately thirty-five new courses were developed for the New University, and fifty or more "old" courses, that is, courses that had been underway during the semester, were being adjusted to meet the new situation.[2] Here is a sample: Myths and Symbols of Peace and War; Northwestern, Whither Goest Thou?; The Sociology of Math; Application of Engineering Analysis to Social Problems; The Press and the Strike; Physics and Politics; Draft Resistance Seminar; Pacifism; The Role of the Computer in Society; Food Buying Co-ops; Toward a Psychology of Conscious Values; Persuasion and Social Agitation. Entire departments, such as sociology and history, became frameworks for anti-war action and research. The role of scholar and activist merged painlessly and the communal euphoria and breakdown of barriers between teacher and pupil were exciting to watch. Everyone, it seemed, was hoping it would carry on into the following autumn. It was truly a community in the finest sense of the word. But it lasted only eight days.

The strike also culminated in other "victories": denial of credit for Naval ROTC courses in the College of Arts and Sciences (the other colleges of the school did not take away credit); the stock portfolio of the university was officially opened for inspection (it seemed *all* the stocks were war-related in one way or another); and the computer center announced

---

[2] For a more detailed description of the New University and other strike activities at Northwestern, see the eye-witness report of Cottle (1970:19-28).

that there was no military classified research being undertaken by the university. These were some of the demands. As Jack Sawyer, professor of sociology and psychology, said in a post-strike letter to the *Daily*: "The revolution didn't happen last week and those who thought it might must have been disappointed. But 80 percent business as usual—if that is where we are—is better than 100 percent business as usual. It is a first step . . ."

If then, there were successes, why is it claimed that, effectively speaking, the strike was a failure? If demands are met, and some were successfully met, then how does failure arise?

First off, it must be emphasized that from the radical perspective, nothing less than the complete sharing of power would do. Short term gains and reforms simply was not acceptable.

The original intent of the strike was to protest the incursion into Cambodia, to reallocate American resources from military involvement abroad to domestic problems here in America, and (after May 4) to protest the deaths of four students at Kent State. The local issues at Northwestern were added later, and it is important to note that the New University was not suggested as a goal until two or three days into the strike. The goals, or at least the original goals, centered around anti-war protest and re-orienting the resources of the society. Needless to say, the protest did not end the war, nor were resources allocated differently since the strike.

It then can be argued as Professor Sawyer said that "it is only the first step," and that these goals must be met in the future. Then the task of the strike was to develop coherent structures with and within which to bring about significant change in a society in which existing institutions have "stogified" and have become unresponsive to the existing needs, or to turn to the other side of the coin, where the normative and evaluative systems of society have changed to such an extent that the evaluative underpinnings of institutions are not held by the people. In this situation, the people hold a very different interpretation of what the institutions should be.

In the student strike, neither a lasting institutional change was effected nor was a firm continuing structure built to carry on protest and change. This is believed to be one aspect of the failure of the Northwestern strike, and in so far as this strike was a microcosm of the national strike, it was a failure of the national strike. The other key aspect of failure was to clearly define the goals of the strike. Furthermore, the orientation of action was on the basis of ad hoc goals and policies which could in no way move effectively toward a redefinition of the microcosm—the university, or the macrocosm—the society.

So then the strike failed both in terms of its own internal logic and vis à vis the society from which it arose. At base, this was due to organizational failure and failure to mobilize long-range support above and beyond the situational and the transient. The strike began as a groundswell—the shoulder shrug of Jacques Bonhomme that Hugo spoke of in France prior to 1789. In this, Kent and Cambodia were simply the *issues* of protests, not the goals to be sought. So initially there was protest and symbolic action rather than a change in actual conditions. Later in the next phase, the local issues were brought forth. When these were met or found to be inapplicable, a vacuum occurred. If there are no more goals, no more windmills to joust, what do you do? After the heady brew of victory, what next? This gap was evidenced when Miss Jefferson, by now the "supreme" leader, would ask the crowds of demonstrators as well as her own co-workers: Just what are our goals now? As Miss Jefferson told one of us during a meeting, "We just can't keep having rallies; the people are getting bored." It was also noted that there was a continually decreasing attendance at rallies and that interest was waning.

The emphasis on "do your own thing" which was in fact a *stated* program from the very beginning and was often announced by the strike leadership, created a conflict of goals and reduced coherency of action to almost nil. Some people began to ask when it would be over. Finally the vote was taken on May 13. There were three choices: to continue striking, to build the New University, or to go back to regular classes and "business as usual." The vote was overwhelmingly to implement the New University.

However, SDS and other radical groups declared fraud because they believed that the New University and the strike were the same. Their attempts at stopping the vote were squelched by Miss Jefferson and the steering committee because she wanted to keep all factions united and to attempt the building of the New or Alternative University, knowing full well that it may mean that it could be co-opted by the administration and that the "fire could burn out," in a sense.

The disgruntled radicals were angry. They had kept in the background of the strike by letting the liberal middle "do its thing." Cynicism is the radicals' secret weapon. Their disagreement with the liberal leadership was sub rosa throughout the strike, but a day after the strike was officially ended, 150 SDSers and other radicals attempted to remove "war material"—files and papers from the offices of the ROTC commanders who were in fact in the process of leaving the building anyway. The police were called in for the first time during the entire strike and 35 students were arrested. The next day (May 14), some 1,200 students plus the Dean of Students approved a Grand Jury investigation before any disciplinary judicial system sentenced them. However, administration pressure killed the investigation and the students were summarily tried and found guilty. The radicals had "tested" the sincerity of the university and found it wanting. The administration still kept all the power. The administration did not want a New University to arise from the old. They did not like the idea of the new politicized nature of the university. They saw the SDS action not as part of the new anti-war perspective of the New University, but as simply an act of vandalism and would be treated as such. As an SDS flyer stated:

> So far the alternative university exists only in our heads and in impotent committees. And the old university administration continues to hide the real issues. . . . By indicting 35 students, the . . . administration has voided the principles of an open anti-war community. . . . Our alternative university is a farce!

All facets of the counter-culture, including the Alternative or New University are "experimental" in a real sense. The trouble with experiments is that people continue to view them only as experiments and will not institutionalize them as ongoing and legitimate structures. Since the university saw the strike as temporary, since many students and faculty (except a vocal minority) did not have the faith (or energy) to make these experiments a definite part of the structure of the university, and since the administration and most of the faculty made no attempt to institutionalize them and give them long-range legitimacy, the strike, the Alternative University, and all the innovative programs and ideas were doomed to fail from the very beginning.

* * *

It would be appropriate to examine more closely the strike actions and their political implications. The actions that took place from May 5 to 12 can be broken down into three categories:

1. Actions that influenced the national political system or a local segment of it, not including the university community.

2. Actions that influenced the university political and sociological community.

3. Actions which affect neither directly, but fall into fringe areas. Included in this category are ritualistic actions, such as songs, chants or ceremonies.

It is ironic, but not surprising, that the first category is smallest, with reference to the strike. Actions that influenced the outside system would include the trip to Washington, the lobbying at the Illinois Congressional Session, the leafletting and distributing petitions in the Evanston community, and writing letters to congressmen. One would assume that to produce a result on the Indochina War or the policy of sending National Guardsmen to campuses, an effect would be needed on the national system. But the majority of strikers were too young to vote, denied the access of an up-coming election (during the strike) and cast out of the main stream (middle class) because of alienating sub-cultural preferences. In short the students with the longest hair had doors slammed in their faces. While the strike was a protest to international and national events it affected these events the least.

Nationally, there was an apparency of student unity and force. This is opposed to the reality of unity, which is, at best, ephemeral. This is not to say that this apparency did not have its effect: it succeeded in causing a limit to be set to the time U.S. troops were to remain in Cambodia (Cambodia became Vietnamized) and secondly, it moved the President to create a study commission on students (for which Miss Jefferson eventually testified). The glaring failures of the strike overrode any apparent successes. U.S. policy in Southeast Asia was not changed and basic conditions in this racist society went unchanged and unheeded. As one Northwestern sociologist stated: "The strike moved history forward one inch, that's all."

It must be mentioned that the strike had an indirect psychological effect on the nation. But this effect is difficult to measure, particularly since it was filtered through the media to a large group who never saw the strike, the American public. Although the strike itself was an expression of anger, it cannot be considered as an action carried on within the larger political system. In fact, it was partially a rejection of the larger system. Acts such as the "secession from the union" are representative of the feeling that strikers did not want to be a part of a system that sanctioned killing in Indochina and Kent, Ohio.

By far, the greatest number of strike actions were carried on within the university political community. The strike began as a reaction to an international event and a national event; then the focus changed to local problems, such as the closing of the administration building and the opening of the stock portfolio. While students were angry about Kent State, they at first could only tell each other. Many university administrators were not around, and many local residents had heard the "true" story from the local papers, and many didn't want to be bothered by students.

Many participants remarked that Northwestern seemed finally to have become a community. This was probably true. The weather was warm enough for people to congregate in numerous informal groups, the campus was isolated from outside traffic and mail, and there was much more contact with other members of the university community. For the first time, departments, living units, and age groups were randomly mixed. If felt truly like a separate "state."

During the strike many more political action committees met and discussed issues. Not mentioned in the account of strike activities are the numerous committee and department meetings that took place every day on all levels. The community also voted on three occasions, and rallied nearly every day. Most plans were made in small group meetings by strike coalitions, but the rubber stamp of the larger academic community was needed in order to preserve the feeling of unity and democracy. Such feelings were present. Strikers believed that they were avenging the deaths of the Kent State four and the pomposity of the Federal government. In reality, the whole community was going on a "rebellion trip," similar to a drug experience and complete with ups and downs.

Also numerous were actions that were planned to maintain interest in the strike, to increase the activities of the participants and to satisfy psychological needs. These activities included the campus newspaper, the strike newspaper, the campus radio station, the burning of dummies, the camp fires, the candle light march, and the strike costumes. The symbolism of protest has been somewhat diffused by its contact with the larger society. So special strike symbols were needed to convince everyone that something different really was happening. Those symbols included the barricade, a red fist clenched, and red armbands. (Later, different colored armbands came to mean different things. Members of the press, for instance, were given blue armbands.) The strike costume consisted of blue jeans, a blue working shirt with a red fist and the word strike printed on the back, and sometimes a red headband.

Perhaps the most ritualistic activities were the evening rallies in which some participants sang songs, danced and listened to presentations that were emotional and artistic in nature. One was reminded of the November 15 Moratorium in Washington, D.C., in which these activities also took place. It is clear that these components functioned to produce solidarity and identification with the group. They also served to set apart the strikers from the rest of the world.

Although the strike was apparently a protest against American democracy and the "silent majority," the decision-making apparatus was modeled after the national system. Decisions began in small meeting rooms with representatives from different factions. This was called the central strike committee. Then they were presented to the large group, discussed and voted upon. The minority of anti-strike students were listened to no more than the strikers themselves were listened to by the American public, and perhaps less.

Actions attempting to influence the public were based on the American public's role as the electorate. Petitions were distributed and the electorate was "influenced" by educating them as to the real facts on Cambodia and Kent State. While President Nixon was calling for unity among the American people, strike leaders were calling for unity among the university community against the Nixon administration.

The political action was termed a "strike," which bears more relevance to an economic structure than a political one. But the students had been educated to believe that when a group doesn't get what it wants, it goes on strike. At numerous times, it was admitted that the strike was only the beginning, and that what was really needed was a longer "campaign" for peace.

A strike public relations effort was made. First, students attempted to explain to the public what was going on. When residents replied, "I know what's going on, I read the papers," students attempted to affect the media. One group of students founded a "Peace News Service," which produced news stories about political actions on campus and sent them to such sources as Associated Press, United Press International, the Chicago papers, and several other media. Another group formed a "watchdog" committee, to monitor the media for bad publicity.

This list could continue for pages, but *the point is that almost every strike action had its parallel in the larger political system.* The actions were based on values of equality and freedom of speech. Ritualism was borrowed and improvised. Values of such things as use of the media, the "rap" (or discussion) group and the "do your own thing" ethos were carried from the larger youth culture into the strike culture.

Whenever social structures operate so as to isolate naturally individuals or groups with the same political outlook from contact with those who have different views, this isolation tends to back political extremism. While the strike was not an insurrection, it manifested more leftist activity than did the preceding winter or the following summer, or the following fall. This might explain the wide degree of interest in the strike. When massed together, the student community is acted upon by certain sociological forces which also apply to the larger setting, the nation. But because students are more prone to questioning the values they have brought with them from home, some values are discarded. Students have accepted the reverse of the belief that the United States is the protector of democracy in the world. The university community is a particular example of the role of the intelligentsia; they tend to be physically isolated as well as intellectually alienated from the larger group. When leaving the campus, the separation drops away, and the norms of the larger group must be adhered to. The disagreement that takes place on campus is a function of this tendency. Some students become more isolated from their parents and their backgrounds on campus, while others do not perceive themselves as being different. Arguments result as to which norms should apply, those of the nation or those of the college community.

During the strike, it was possible to mobilize a large number of people who were willing to accept the college norms (particularly the political ones). The invasion of Cambodia gave the strikers an intellectual issue; the killings at Kent gave them an emotional force. Because the group became solidified, it began acting in accordance with the adjusted college values, but at the same time realized that it had separated itself.

It is interesting to note the disgust that uninvolved observers expressed for the behavior produced by the new norms. One *Chicago Tribune* reporter wrote about a student pot-party celebration during the strike, strongly implying that "if those kids were going to have a protest, they'd better be damn serious about it."

Legitimacy involves the capacity of the system to engender and maintain the belief that the existing political institutions are the most appropriate ones for society. The extent to which contemporary democratic political systems are legitimate depends upon the ways in which the key issues which have historically divided the society are resolved.

While young strikers were attempting to express that they felt the Nixon administration was illegitimate, the larger community was reacting negatively to the striker's actions, based on their own values. The strikers had evaluated the war and found the way it had been dealt with illegitimately. The public evaluated the actions of the young rebels and found *them illegitimate*. And most of the judging was affected by emotional factors.

It will probably be some time before such a strike happens again, if it ever does. The participants in the action had much higher expectations for the results of the strike, and many have slipped into a cycle of apathy as a result of this disillusionment. But it is highly probable that students will strike again, given time to become further alienated from their society.

REFERENCES

Cottle, Thomas J. "Strike Week in Chicago." *Change Magazine* 2 (July-August): 19-28, 1970.

Chapter V
ROTC: Pro and Con

The shootings at Kent State culminated nearly a decade of student protest. At Northwestern the strike in early May of 1970 brought the issue of ROTC to an end. On May 9, 1970, SDS led its last anti-ROTC rally. Ten days later, on May 19, the faculty of the College of Arts and Sciences voted to take away all credit from ROTC courses. One event was *not* the cause and effect of the other. The CAS vote was the result of a year long debate; it is fairly likely that the CAS would have taken away credit even if Kent State had never occurred. It was, however, the final "push."

These are the bare facts, but the question arises: what were the differing attitudes and ideologies of the participants at Northwestern? How did the students, faculty, and administration feel about ROTC? By examining these attitudes, both pro and con, we will see how complex the situation is and how different action (or lack of action) took place. Nearly *one month* before the events surrounding Kent State took place, this author's questionnaire was analyzed; *two weeks* before Kent State, Northwestern held a referendum on the Vietnam War and on the status of ROTC. Thus the killings and the strike did not contaminate the attitudes of students and faculty. The results of these findings showed how split the students were on the status of ROTC.

THE STUDENT REFERENDUM

On April 14, 1970, Northwestern held its election for student government.[1] As part of the ballot, referendum on the status of ROTC was held, as well as a question on Vietnam. It was the largest turn-out for an election in NU's history. The voter total of 3,459 represented more than half of NU's undergraduates. Table 4 shows the results of that referendum as compared to the results of the author's mailed questionnaire.[2] The NU student body was split three ways: 27 percent favored what can be called the "radical position," the immediate removal and abolishment of ROTC; the "liberal position," ROTC can stay on campus as an extracurricular activity but with no credit, accounted for 32 percent; and the "conservative position," the status-quo position, that ROTC remains as it is, on campus and with credit reflected 41 percent of the students. The students were divided three ways and each position could present a strong argument that its position represented the majority.[3] For example, 59 percent did oppose credit for ROTC courses, that is when one combines the radical and liberal position, yet 41 percent voted to retain the ROTC program, a sizable and impressive minority. It becomes more impressive when one also notes that 75 percent of the students voted to

---

[1] This election was interesting in that, for the first time in NU's history, two Blacks were running for president of the associated student government. One represented the Interests of Greeks, the other the "independents" on campus. The latter won.

[2] The author had a hand in developing the referendum questions and tried to get six choices for the status of ROTC. Instead, only three were allowed on the ballot. The three, "remove ROTC from campus," "ROTC stays, but should receive no credit," and "ROTC remains as it is," were a regrouping of the six choices used on the author's questionnaire. Thus, one can see the similarity in responses when choices 1 and 2 are combined, 3 and 4, and so on. This similarity showed not only that my synthesis "worked" but also pointed out that the questionnaire, in still another way, was a valid reflection of student attitudes. (For more on this, see Methodology section in back.)

[3] Compare the divisiveness over the ROTC question to the one on Vietnam. Clearly, Vietnam was a more polarized issue. The referendum asked: "Should the U.S. immediately pull its troops out of Vietnam?" The answer was unequivocal: seventy-five percent of the students said "yes" to the question, twenty-five percent said "no."

keep the ROTC unit on campus, that is the combination of the liberal and conservative position. These figures were not simply statistical juggling; they served as a basis for debate within faculty and administration discussions in order to win points for one side or another. For example, in an argument before the Faculty Senate, two professors, Richard B. Heflebower and A. Louis Allred, made the following plea in support of ROTC:

> You do not reunite the campus by overriding the wishes of 41 percent of the students on an issue which men of goodwill can honestly disagree and, in the bargain, deprive 160 students (the ROTC cadets on campus) of their freedom to participate in a program that 73 percent of the students and a majority of the university faculty have endorsed.

Thus, the referendum did affect policy-making: it helped counteract the radical protest during that year by showing the actual feelings of students on the issue, plus it solidified the final policy of *the* most important decision-making body on campus (at least vis a vis ROTC): the Faculty Senate. The Senate's decision was to keep ROTC on campus; jurisdiction over credit would lay in the hands of each separate school or college on campus. Let us now look at each of the student positions and the rationale behind them.

THE RADICAL PERSPECTIVE

As Table 5 shows, 50 percent of those who labeled themselves radical picked choice number one, and statistically, the median choice was also number one: the immediate removal of ROTC. For radicals, faculty as well as students, the issue is not debatable; it is not academic; it is not a question of credit; it is not a question that ROTC may provide a group of officers who are more liberal than those trained in schools like West Point. There is no moral distinction between a liberal killer and a dogmatic killer. They are the same in the eyes of radicals. But the radical position transcends the issue of ROTC. For radicals, ROTC is a political issue, not an academic one; it is a symbol of political repression at home and economic imperialism abroad, particularly in Vietnam and the rest of Southeast Asia. The following quote, taken from probably the

TABLE 4

STUDENT REFERENDUM COMPARED TO QUESTIONNAIRE

	April 1, 1970 Questionnaire (N = 257)			April 14, 1970 Student Referendum (N = 3,459)
The radical position:				
Choice #1	16%	> 26%	Remove ROTC from campus	27%
Choice #2	10			
The liberal position:				
Choice #3	16	> 33%	ROTC stays, but no credit	32%
Choice #4	17			
The conservative position:				
Choice #5	26	> 41%	ROTC remains as it is	41%
Choice #6	15			
	100%			100%

CHOICES

Choice #1 NROTC should be immediately removed from campus and abolished as a campus activity.

Choice #2 NROTC should be phased out slowly by not bringing in any future participants into the program.

Choice #3 NROTC should be made an off-campus, extracurricular, no-credit activity.

Choice #4 NROTC courses should be available to any student on campus but should carry no academic credit.

Choice #5 NROTC courses carrying academic credit should be taught on campus, but under a separate department not affiliated with the College of Arts and Sciences.

Choice #6 NROTC courses, carrying academic credit, should be taught within the College of Arts and Sciences.

most articulate position paper on ROTC and written by Harvard SDS, points out the larger issue:

> The abolition of ROTC on the Harvard campus is imperative not because ROTC maintains low academic standards, but because the policies its men defend and the interests they serve are fundamentally wrong.
>
> Some people think that American policy in Vietnam has been misguided (and perhaps even immoral in the use of napalm, etc.) but that now, America's leaders are slowly becoming "reasonable." We disagree. We think that the Vietnam policy has always been harmoniously integrated in the larger pattern of the American government's aims and interests around the world and here at home. Vietnam is not an isolated mistake! (Harvard SDS Collective, 1969:2)

TABLE 5

ATTITUDES TOWARD ROTC BY THE POLITICAL VIEWS OF NU STUDENTS

	Radical Students (N=49)	Liberal Students (N=149)	Conservative Students (N=59)	All Students (N=257)
Choice #1	50%	10%	6%	16%
Choice #2	15	11	0	10
Choice #3	17	22	6	16
Choice #4	12	19	17	17
Choice #5	4	31	34	26
Choice #6	2	8	38	15
	100%	101%	101%	100%

	Choice #1 (N=41)	Choice #2 (N=26)	Choice #3 (N=42)	Choice #4 (N=45)	Choice #5 (N=67)	Choice #6 (N=36)
Radical	56%	33%	19%	14%	5%	5%
Liberal	35	68	74	64	68	36
Conservative	9	0	7	22	28	59
	100%	101%	100%	100%	101%	100%

Source: Author's mailed questionnaire, Northwestern University, Spring 1970.

The logic behind this position is as follows: people are followers of tradition, and tend to be fooled by others who claim to follow tradition (like the president of the United States). They fail to think for themselves and must be educated to realize the problems of the world, either through logical appeals or through emotional sympathy for those who dedicate their lives to societal betterment.

The war in Vietnam is wrong because killing is immoral and the United States has no right to be a "world policeman." There is much poverty and racial strife in this country that should be taken care of first, and furthermore, the U.S. intervenes in the affairs of other countries not out of good will, but to protect its economic and political interests. The latter is defined as imperialism.

It is not necessary to maintain so large a standing army simply for defense. This "defense" in actuality promotes world suspicion, causes increased stock-piling of weapons, and threatens nuclear war. In fact, the need for this "defense" is invented by high-level members of the military, the Pentagon, and the corporate structure who have their own interests in mind, either military or economic, and not simply the protection of the country. The armed forces are then a tool to protect the imperialistic interests of the U.S.

ROTC generally, the Naval ROTC in particular on the campus, is really a local training branch of the United States armed forces and, therefore, is part of the imperialist "machine." Former SDS president, Jeff Rice, put it this way in an interview:

> The armed forces of the United States are currently being used as an agent of repression both here and abroad. The ROTC on campus is actively feeding this agent of repression and, therefore, must cease such complicity with these activities. By fighting for abolishing ROTC, one then confronts not only Vietnam but manifestations of American imperialism on campus, such as biological research, counter-insurgency research, etc. It is a means of confrontation by using the university as a base for operations.

Finally, the only way to effect real change and improve the system is to "destroy" it and replace it with a better one, and to do this, violence is necessary. This, in capsule form, is the basis for the radical perspective.

THE LIBERAL PERSPECTIVE

The liberal perspective is exemplified by choices three or four. (See Table 4 or 5). The median choice of those who labeled themselves "liberals" was choice number four: NROTC courses should be available to students but should carry no academic credit. This position was also the median one chosen by all students. This was true when sex was held constant, but there was a difference when membership in a fraternity or sorority was correlated: the median choice for "non-Greeks" was the "liberal" position, number four. For "Greeks," the median was choice number five, a conservative position. This came as no surprise; it again pointed out that fraternity-sorority members, though in a process of change, still opt for the status-quo. The liberal position was a position that centered on two areas: freedom of choice and academic "goodness." These same areas were also ones that deeply concerned the faculty and eventually affected *their* decisions regarding ROTC. The liberal position, because of its broad scope, touched on both the radical and conservative positions, as Table 6 shows, and its logic was as follows:[4]

People are basically good but tend to be misled by traditions and by individuals good at disguising their real motives (like the President). If these people could be shown how the world could be a better place, most would cooperate. Through reason and fair play, such cooperation is possible.

The war in Vietnam is wrong because we are killing ideologically motivated people simply because their beliefs differ from ours. We have no right to be in Vietnam especially when there is so much poverty, racism and ecological problems right here in the United States. While it may be necessary to main-

---

[4] This, in retrospect, proved a weakness in the survey. Future research should break down "liberal" into three areas: left-liberal, liberal, and "middle of the road." This may facilitate analysis of the liberal position.

tain an army to defend this country, it should be smaller, on a volunteer basis, and should not be so costly.

ROTC should not offer academic credit because it is a part of the armed forces, and not a legitimate academic field. The right of individuals to join ROTC should not be regulated by others, however. Credit should be taken away, but students should have the right to take ROTC courses and keep their ROTC scholarships.

Furthermore, ROTC does liberalize the armed forces by providing officers with a broad educational background. The removal of ROTC programs would tend to isolate the military officer corps and greatly increase the prospect of a powerful, ingrown military elite.

Finally, it is morally incorrect to use violence to achieve change. There are many peaceful means of protest, and these should be the means to a better society.

THE CONSERVATIVE PERSPECTIVE

The median choice for those labeling themselves conservatives was choice number five: ROTC should stay on campus, with credit, but under a separate department not affiliated with the College of Arts and Sciences. This was essentially the view of the administration's official stance (the Chancellor in particular) and the view of the Faculty Senate. It was more than a "view"; it was what eventually happened to ROTC, with one exception: credit was taken away by the CAS. In short, it was not a clear-cut "victory" for anyone. The logic behind the conservative position was essentially this: leave the issue in the hands of the authorities; in this case, the Faculty Senate and the Chancellor. A small vocal group (SDS) has no right to impose its views on any individual or group on campus. It is this libertarian aspect of conservatism, the individual rights of students, that comes into direct conflict with the radical assumption that even a minority position has a moral right to infringe upon others.

The conservative perspective assumes that people are followers of tradition and that leaders of nation-states (like the president of the United States) follow traditions that are in the best interests of the people. These leaders have the expertise and the power to make such decisions and should be respected and followed.

The war in Vietnam is correct because, one, we have been invited to protect a nation, and two, we must defend that nation and ourselves from Communist aggression, and protect our own political and economic interests. It is necessary, therefore, to have a standing army to protect such interests. ROTC is an important part of such a standing army since it supplies officers that are necessary for the maintenance of such an army.

ROTC has several advantages: first, it is a source of volunteers for the armed forces, and we support ROTC because we support an all-volunteer military. Secondly, ROTC gives many students the opportunity to attend college who otherwise would not be able to attend college at all by providing scholarships to needy students.[5] Thirdly, ROTC provides an armed force that is more representative, both economically and educationally, of the nation as a whole. Fourth, the civilian-soldier concept of ROTC would help insure that the military remain completely apolitical and would help avoid an elite military caste.

Furthermore, one must condemn violence that destroys university property and intimidates students, faculty, and administrators. Such action is totalitarian and must be dealt with severely.

As one conservative student put it:

> Any student or group of students which seeks to appoint itself censor of university curriculum, that condones violence, and seeks to subvert the foreign policy democratically agreed

---

[5] Those who oppose ROTC claim they are not against individual ROTC students, and they favor substitution of university scholarships for ROTC scholarships. The cost for such a policy would be at least $270,000 at Northwestern alone. In view of its current financial crises, universities simply could not afford such a policy. This view again points out the dependence of American universities on governmental and military sources of money.

upon by the American people, can only be called totalitarian. No one should be forced to take ROTC courses, but neither should anyone be prevented from taking them.

This essentially is the libertarian position of the conservative perspective. The "traditional" position is more hard-line. It dispenses with the reasoned debate and states simply a "love-it-or-leave-it-damn-the-radicals" point of view. It is ready to do battle with the radicals and is outraged that the administration is so "soft" on the issue. It wants firm authority. Its anger against liberal students, faculty, or administrators is almost as great as that directed against radicals.

THE FACULTY PERSPECTIVE

The faculty was as split as the students. No statistical survey was taken to gauge faculty support, but there were as many shades of opinions among the NU faculty as among students. However, the liberal position seemed to be the pivot. Generally, younger professors oppose credit for ROTC courses, while older ones support credit. Older members of the faculty—over 60—support ROTC the way it has existed. Very few members under 40 feel ROTC should get credit. Assistant Professor of sociology, Allan Schnaiberg, was quoted, however, as saying:

> Pro-ROTC support is more heavily weighed toward the older professors, but it is not exclusive by any means. It is not nearly as polarized as some people think.

Since there is only impressionistic evidence and not hard data, it is difficult to make generalizations. But a major sentiment was stated by Associate Journalism Professor Jack Z. Sissors: "Many NU professors—until they get other evidence—like the status quo." But since the issue was raised and new evidence was pointed out, there occurred some change in the status quo. In short, actions spoke louder than words.

The issue of ROTC was debated around two points: one was over accreditation; the other concened the use of university facilities. In short, the academics saw the issue as essentially an academic question, not a political one. If one thing stands out about faculty decision-making, it is that they rarely make rash decisions. For over a year there was debate and discussions, resolutions and compromises. Though spurred by radical students, the debate centered about the liberal and conservative positions. The most volatile reason against ROTC was the radical one: ROTC is seen as an extension of the military-industrial complex and thus must be removed. Few professors, however, accepted that view. When credit was finally removed by the CAS, it was because the professors felt that ROTC courses did not have academic merit. As one professor put it: "ROTC should get as much credit as you get for attending a lecture at Hillel (a campus religious house)." Yet this same professor felt that ROTC should still be able to use campus facilities.

The gist of most of the arguments seemed to be the following: ROTC should stay on campus because armed forces officers need a liberal background that a college can provide. But credit should be thought over carefully by each school in the university. In any case, after much vacillation, credit was eventually restored to four NROTC courses in the spring of 1971. (For a complete description of post-strike decision-making, see the Epilogue.)

In the end, the Faculty Senate voted to keep ROTC on campus because it provided a "broad, liberal background," a committee was appointed to review course offerings and personnel appointments, and credit was to be determined by each school. The College of Arts and Sciences was one school that denied but later returned credit; the other five undergraduate schools (Speech, Music, Journalism, Technological Institute, and Education) have all retained credit. (See Appendix.)

From all this a few summary remarks can be made: first, faculty decisions are usually made slowly and torturously even if students place great urgency upon them; two, it is highly unlikely that the faculty would have acted by itself on such political issues as ROTC. It needed the spur of student protest; third, as in the case of most radical causes, if the radicals succeed, it is because of help from liberals—who act out of different motives than radicals; and last, the faculty emerged as a key decision-maker, showing more power in the case of ROTC than the administration.

THE ADMINISTRATION'S PERSPECTIVE

As was pointed out earlier, many key administrators have close personal and professional ties to the military. For example, at Northwestern, the Chancellor, the past chief counsel to the university, and several members of the Board of Trustees, were officers in the Navy, including at least one admiral. Thus, for personal reasons alone, the chief administrators wanted to see Naval ROTC remain as it was. Officially, the Chancellor went along with the final decisions of the Faculty Senate and the College of Arts and Sciences. Privately, he disagreed with the elimination of credit. The President of the University, Robert Strotz, was happy with the final decision. One point must be mentioned though: Strotz, during the debate within CAS, was at the time dean of that college and presided over the meetings. In short, there was little that the administration could do except put informal pressure on the deans of each school; it could not influence the voting pattern of each professor, since essentially ROTC was a faculty decision to make. Each school had the power to decide on credit, and the Faculty Senate could decide the status of ROTC on campus, particularly whether the contract between the university and the Department of Defense should be continued, and if yes, how should military courses and faculty appointments of Navy officers be approved. In the end, the administration was relatively happy over the results.

The final outcome was historically familiar to the administration. For many years, scholars, not only at Northwestern but at all colleges where ROTC existed, who were sympathetic to the goals of ROTC had been recommending similar reforms.[6] Such Such reforms in the past served to make ROTC more legitimate and academically acceptable.

---

[6] For a history of how ROTC has adapted to university reform of courses, personnel, and financing, see Gene M. Lyons and John W. Masland, *Education and Military Leadership: A Study of ROTC* (1959).

CONCLUSION

The ways of academic procedure are deeply puzzling, even to an insider. The university is a confederation of many interest groups. There are a maze of committees. There are so many points of view.[7] Yet any theory of decision-making must take into account two very important variables that profoundly affect the role of participants in campus protest and help explain how a set of attitudes propel one into action. One can be called, for lack of a better term, *consciousness,* the other is organizational *constraints.*

Consciousness will be defined as a reflective mental attitude enabling an individual to become aware of himself and his environment in various degrees of clarity and complexity. This consciousness has to do with the awareness of the individual of himself, his social groups or class, and his society.[8] It would take an entire book to describe how consciousness is formed, but several ways should be mentioned: one's family influence, one's peer group influence, one's reading habits, one's status and role in an organization, and one's self-awareness. By means of all these influences, one's consciousness is formed. Within a complex organization like the university, there are many groups representing various levels of consciousness. In this study, it is political consciousness one is interested in, and in particular, one's view of ROTC and ROTC protest.

---

[7] Two views that were not mentioned but that should be in any analysis of student protest are that of the maintenance personnel, the campus workers, and that of the staff, the secretarial and kindred office workers. They are usually left of the picture. The workers have to clean up and patch up the damage of student protest; the secretarial staff has to undertake the "paper work" that inevitably flows from such protest. The workers are not all "hard-hat" Wallace-voting types. Many sympathize with student demands. Many, of course, are tired of patching up broken windows and removing revolutionary slogans off walls. On some campuses, SDS has even attempted coalitions with workers for higher wages and more benefits. At Harvard and the University of Chicago, there was some success in this area. Office workers, like most white-collar workers, have been nearly impossible to organize.

[8] For further elaboration of how the social influences the self, see George Herbert Mead (1934).

When radical students talk about raising political consciousness, this is meant to mean the raising of insight, to see the issue of ROTC in global political terms, e.g. complicity with the armed forces in Vietnam, complicity with the military-industrial complex, complicity with political-economic imperialism abroad. The role of all protest is not only to "raise the issue," but to raise consciousness. When there is resistance to such efforts, there is conflict. The three broad aggregates of radical, liberal, and conservative students all have varied and conflicting levels of consciousness. Radical students and liberal-conservative faculty also have conflicting levels of consciousness. Even faculty and administration have conflict due to such differences.

If one were a Marxist, one could introduce the concept of class-consciousness, the process whereby the members of a class become "aware" of themselves as a collective identity and destiny. The radical SDS perspective takes the view that the chief administrators and the board of trustees represent a highly privileged class that "oppresses" other classes. Radicals, though some may have also come from this very same privileged class, have become déclassé and sympathize with the "oppressed" classes, whether they be workers or Blacks. Another view sees *all* students as a "class" with a common identity and destiny, and they too are "oppressed" by a privileged class. This Marxian perspective has strong points and weaknesses. The board of trustees and the chief administrators are members of an elite class. However, faculty and students do not fit neatly into this scheme. In the case of ROTC, it is the faculty that was the major decision-maker. What are the class-interests of the faculty? Outside the Marxist context, the term class-consciousness may be used in an operational sense to denote a "high" degree of sharing of attitudes of isolation, solidarity, and collective purpose within a national subgroup, most of whose members also share a common set of skills, relation to the means of production, and style of life. This then can describe faculty members quite well. It can also describe students.

But there are differences of opinion within the faculty and the students and between them. And there are the organizational constraints mentioned earlier. Students have really three options: to do nothing and accept what is decided by the faculty, to protect their grievances peacefully, or to protest them violently. They do *not* have decision-making powers. The faculty does, but believes itself constrained to decide only academic issues or issues from an academic point of view. This is what it did in the case of ROTC. The CAS was constrained to view the issue, at most, from the point of view of credit. The Faculty Senate could have done more; it could have abolished ROTC. It did not because the political consciousness of the majority of faculty felt ROTC should stay on campus. It could not do more, e.g. get rid of war-related stocks or bonds or end the war in Vietnam. The first it could not do because this is the domain of the chief administrators and the board of trustees; the second it could not do, because it was powerless to do it. Parenthetically, it must be added that some radical demands are either beyond the powers of a university (e.g. ending the WAR) or are economically "suicidal" (e.g. getting rid of war-related stock; so many stocks are war-related, even shoe-strings for army boots).

So these are a few of the constraints that impede action *even if the political consciousness were there.* Consciousness and constraint are intertwined. They both explain the nature of conflict with the organizational setting of the university. A further aspect of the Marxist perspective is that consciousness can change, not as fast as radicals would like, but it can change. Organizationally, the university has the ability to adapt, to move with the events and make adjustments, to be responsive to change. But to many students (and faculty), the machinery is cumbersome and change seems to take place slowly and at great cost to these students and faculty. In this sense, the university seems to characterize the technocratic society as a whole.

REFERENCES

Harvard SDS Collective. *The Case for Abolishing ROTC.* Boston: The New England Free Press, 1969.

Lyons, Gene M. and John W. Masland. *Education and Military Leadership: A Study of ROTC.* Princeton, New Jersey: Princeton University Press, 1959.

Mead, George Herbert. *Mind, Self, and Society.* Chicago: University of Chicago Press, 1934.

Chapter VI
ROTC as Technocratic Symbol

This is a difficult chapter to write. To synthesize the growing literature on the post-industrial technocracy and then to point out how ROTC is a symbol of this technocracy is not easy. Yet the "hook" upon which this entire study is hung, the central thesis, is that ROTC protest is not simply protest directed against the presence of 160 Navy midshipmen on a Midwestern campus but is symbolic of a far more important issue. This study, from the very beginning, has laid down this thesis. The first chapter discussed the university as a corporation and a confederation of various interest-groups—trustees, administrators, and faculty. Student subcultures were then examined in detail, and later, these subcultures were examined as to their views toward ROTC. The history of student protest at Northwestern was examined, not as an isolated series of events, but to show how they were intertwined with national and international affairs. The culmination of nearly a decade of student protest nationally and a year of ROTC protest locally, was pointed out when the strike over Kent State and Cambodia was described. Throughout this book, but especially in the previous chapter, the decision-making processes of the university were examined.

This chapter will attempt to tie together the various strands and weave the central thesis: ROTC as technocratic symbol. To do this, the following questions have to be considered: What is the nature of the technocratic state? What is the nature and role of the military-industrial complex within the technocratic society? What are the connections between the university and the military, between ROTC and the university? Why was ROTC chosen as a symbol of the technocracy? And finally, what conclusions can we draw about future protest within this technocracy? Any one of these questions can, of course, be the basis for an entire book or series of books; thus the descriptions will be brief. If the reader needs more facts and logic to understand these questions, he or she should consult the bibliographic items mentioned in the text.

THE NATURE OF THE TECHNOCRATIC STATE

Whether one calls it the Corporate State (Reich, 1970), the over-live society (Birenbaum, 1969), the technological society (Ellul, 1964), the technocratic society (Roszak, 1969), the technetronic society (Braden, 1970), or the new industrial state (Galbraith, 1967), the point remains that there has emerged since World War II a form of society that mankind has never known. The United States is the most advanced example of such a society, yet it may also be a future model for nearly all highly industrialized nation-states, no matter what their political form of government—socialist, capitalist, or mixed-economies. That it exists in America is unquestioned; that there is a grave concern among social scientists with the implications of technology is unquestioned; that there is a symbiotic relationship between technological change and social change is unquestioned. What has been questioned is the nature of such change and its effect upon the citizens of the technocratic society. Let us first attempt to describe this society by describing what technology is:

> Technology means the systematic application of scientific or other organized knowledge to practical tasks. (Galbraith, 1967: 24)

> . . . we define technology as the organization of knowledge for the achievement of practical purposes. It is in this broader meaning that we can best see the extent and variety of the effects of technology on our institutions and values. Its pervasive influence on our very lives and culture would be unintelligible if technology were understood as no more than machines. (Mesthene, 1970:25)

There are, in a crude fashion, three ways to view technology.[1] One view holds that technology is a virtually unalloyed blessing for man and society, the motor of all progress. It is seen as holding solutions for most of our social problems, as helping to liberate the individual from the clutches of a complex and highly organized society, and as a source of permanent prosperity—in short, as the promise of utopia in our time. On the surface, this view exhibits the optimism that one associates with the rationalistic tradition in western intellectual history, as in eighteenth century Enlightenment in France, for example. It places great faith in the social efficacy of scientific methods and tools. Below the surface, one can, however, detect aspects of economic and political ideology. Vested interests find profit or other advantage in new technology.

A contrary view sees technology as an almost unmitigated curse. Technology is said to rob people of their jobs, their privacy, the participation in democratic government, and, in the end, of their dignity as human beings. It is seen as autonomous and uncontrollable, as fostering materialistic values, as destructive of religion, as bringing about a state in which the individual is increasingly submerged, and threatening to poison nature and blow up the world.

This view is heir to different traditions. On one hand, it is akin to historical "back-to-nature" attitudes toward the world, such as associated with Jean-Jacques Rousseau and Henry Thoreau. It also derives from traditional socialist critiques of the appropriation of technology as capital. If the first view is essentially optimistic, the second is generally pessimistic.

Yet there is a third view, a view that sees technology, not as an autonomous and uncontrollable "machine" nor as a panacea for all of mankind, but as a development that can be harnessed to bring about a high standard of living as well as

---

[1] This section is based in part upon Emmanuel G. Mesthene's book, *Technological Change* (1970:16-20).

give people freedom to develop, grow, and love. This view sees humankind controlling its technology and not being controlled. Yet it is a vision; in reality there exists a technocracy that is quite different. Theodore Roszak gives us one of the best definitions of this state:

> By the technocracy, I mean that social form in which an industrial society reaches the peak of its organizational integration. It is the ideal men usually have in mind when they speak of modernizing, updating, rationalizing, planning. Drawing upon such unquestionable imperatives as the demand for efficiency, for social security, for large-scale coordination of men and resources, for ever higher levels of affluence and ever more impressive manifestations of collective human power, the technocracy works to knit together the anachronistic gaps and fissures of the industrial society. (1969:5)

Such a technocracy reduces man to a technical man, a slave to technique, according to Jacques Ellul. It pervades and knits together nearly all aspects of the society: politics, education, leisure, war-making, entertainment, even the very protest and protesters who fight against it. Let us now examine one of the prime elements, some would say, *the prime* element in the technocracy: the military-industrial complex.

THE MILITARY-INDUSTRIAL COMPLEX

The military-industrial complex that the late President Eisenhower warned the country against in his farewell address in 1960, and that C. Wright Mills so eloquently described in *The Power Elite (1956)* and *The Causes of World War Three* (1958) has become today a mammoth "state within a state." It goes beyond even the "complex" that Eisenhower warned against, which was a loose collaboration of senior military officers, industrial managers, and government legislators tied together mainly through market relations.

Instead, a huge industrial management has been installed in the federal government, under the Secretary of Defense, to control the country's largest network of industrial enterprises. With a characteristic managerial propensity for extending its power, limited only by its allocated share of the gross national product, this new "state-management" combines peak economic, political, and military decision-making. This combination of powers, all under the same roof in the Pentagon, had previously been a feature of American capitalism.[2] The formal, central-management office that administers this military-industrial empire was organized and defined in the early 1960's under the direction of the late President John Kennedy. The man responsible for it all was Robert McNamara, former Secretary of Defense, who modeled this central administrative system on the corporate management model of the Ford Motor Corporation (of which he was once chairman of the board).[3]

This culminated a trend that had been occurring for some time: the civilianization of the military. This central control center, housed in the Pentagon, and in fact, administered by *civilians,* not military personnel, regulated (in 1968) the production of *44 billion dollars* worth of goods and services for military use. This figure is larger than the gross national product of *entire* countries, for example Sweden (a GNP of $21.3 billion) or Italy (a GNP of $61.4 billion). Within this center, there are over 15,000 men and women who arrange work assignments to subordinate managers (contract negotiation), and 40,000 people who oversee compliance of sub-managers of sub-divisions with the top management's rules. This is the largest industrial central administrative office in the United States, perhaps in the world, according to Melman. In fact, the industrial output of this $44 billion worth of goods and services under its control (in 1968) dwarfed the reported net sales of America's leading firms. (For example, General Motors' net sales were $22.8 billion; General Electric, $8.4 billion; A.T.&T., $14.1 billion; U.S. Steel, $4.6 billion; and Dupont $3.4 billion).

This colosseus, combined with huge conglomerate combinations and multi-national corporations, has made the United

---

[2] It is what Seymour Melman (1970) calls "Pentagon capitalism." See also Adam Yarmolinsky's book, *The Military Establishment* (1971) for another sober picture of the military.
[3] For documentation of this, see Melman (1970:1-7). The figures that follow are also from Melman (1970:2,4,7).
[4] For a more complete description of the corporation and its national and international power, see Barber (1970), Zeitlin (1970), Trebing (1970), Galbraith (1967), and Servan-Schreiber (1968).

States the strongest economic power in the world.[4] With the vast network of a military ready to defend these economic interests, the United States has become the greatest neo-imperialist power in the world. As Melman so succinctly summarizes this phenomenon:

> Clearly, no mere ideology or desire for personal power can account for the colossal costs of the military machine. A lust for power has been at work here, but it is not explicable in terms of an individual's power drive. Rather, the state-management represents a power lust . . . an unprecedented ability and opportunity for building a military-iendustry empire at home and for using this as an instrument for building an empire abroad. *This is the new imperialism.* (1970:4, emphasis added.)

THE UNIVERSITY AND THE MILITARY: THE CASE OF ROTC

When one talks about a military-industrial complex, one must now add the university to this complex. Universities occupy an extremely important role in the technocratic society. They are centers for producing new knowledge, educating men and women to wield this knowledge, and doing research that is essential to the security of the society. As has been shown in the introduction, the American universities since World War II have undergone a transformation; they have been welded to the military-industrial complex in three important ways: (a) counterinsurgency work,[5] (b) military

---

[5] The CIA network is extensive. It recruits students directly from the universities. The Ivy League schools have always been a source of CIA employees. For instance, the dean of students at Princeton and the former treasurer of Yale were recruiters. It manipulates students in the National Student Association, especially at international student conferences. Two of its biggest scandals were "Project Camelot," a research project aimed at quelling communist revolutions in South America by using social scientists to study and simulate actual conditions. The CIA usually works through "fronts"; in the latter case, the CIA "front" was the American University's Center of Research in Social Systems (CRESS). The list can go on, and are all amply documented in Ridgeway's book (1968:120-131).

(defense, biological, chemical warfare) research,[6] and (c) military training (ROTC). It is no wonder that universities, especially the most prestigious ones, have been targets of student protest; the academic cloister of the past has become so "militarized" that the Founding Fathers would not recognize it.

This transformation has been documented elsewhere. Clark Kerr, the ex-Chancellor at Berkeley, details it in his book *The Uses of the University* (1963); James Ridgeway has written a alliance with the university, *The Closed Corporation* (1968), and David Horowitz's articles in *Ramparts* Magazine (1969) is also an important contribution in this area. The universities have become primary centers for work in basic science as well as technology, and federal money to support them has become a major factor in the total performance of these universities. Kerr (1963:53) notes that higher education in 1960 received $1.5 billion from the federal government—a hundredfold increase in twenty years; about two-thirds of this, or $1 billion, went for research. Melman (1970:97-98) continues to

---

[6] Military research in a wide variety of areas goes on at numerous campuses. For example, the University of California's Radiation Laboratory in Livermore and Los Alamos (New Mexico) designs and builds prototypes of H-bombs; MIT and Johns Hopkins run centers which design missiles; half of MIT's budget and three-quarters of Johns Hopkins' budget comes from running defense labs; MIT, for example, received $119 million from the Pentagon in fiscal year 1968—27 percent of all the research spending by this state management in American universities; Johns Hopkins received $57 million; Cornell designs more effective bombs for use in Vietnam; Princeton breaks codes and even runs conventions for the CIA; Michigan is first in photo reconnaissance; Pennsylvania and fifty other universities have been involved in chemical, germ, and biological warfare research; Cornell's Aeronautical Laboratory helped Johns Hopkins design an early Bumblebee missile for the Navy, then went on to the design work for the Army's Lacrosse missile; Princeton and the University of California—Davis does research on how to defoliate trees, presumably for use in Vietnam; the University of Pittsburgh's Washington office is noted for studying new methods to improve tank gun sights; the University of Rochester in upstate New York manages the Secret Center for Naval Analysis in Alexandria, Virginia. The list can go on and on and again is documented in Ridgeway (1967:111-136) and Melman (1970:97-106). Northwestern, incidentally, does engage in research under military contracts, but states that it is neither classified nor dealing with chemical-biological warfare.

point out that in 1966-67, this grew to $1.3 billion; though only *ten percent* of total federal support for research and development, accounted for 75 *percent* of all university expenditures on research and 15 percent of total university budgets. Kerr breaks this down and states that for fiscal year 1961, the Department of Defense, the Atomic Energy Commission, and the National Aeronautics and Space Administration combined to provide 41 percent of all federal research funds to universities. (The Department of Defense alone provided 32 percent or one-third of *all* funds.) The other agencies to pour money into research were the Department of Health, Education, and Welfare, particularly, the National Institute of Health (39%); the National Science Foundation (11%); and the Department of Agriculture (6%).[7] Thus, we see that the Pentagon—Department of Defense and its allied agencies account for nearly *half* of all federally sponsored research.

Let us now take the case of ROTC. Besides providing research, the universities also provide an inexpensive (to the Pentagon) means of training officers for the American military. The partnership between the universities and ROTC goes back to the Morrill Land Grant Act of 1862.[8] Representative Justin Morrill of Vermont, when advocating the passage of the Land Grant Act, proposed that military education be incorporated in the bill. Of course, long prior to the passage of the Morrill Act, there had been military colleges to provide trained officers;

---

[7] These figures all come from Kerr (1963:53). These figures do not include funds for university-operated government research centers. If they did, the 41 percent would climb even higher.

[8] This section on ROTC and the universities is based on a sixty-one page document privately distributed by the Department of Defense and compiled by its Special Committee on ROTC. This report which examined the history, curriculum, faculty and *raison d'être* of ROTC was approved and accepted by Secretary of Defense Melvin Laird and his assistant Roger T. Kelley. The report maintained that ROTC should remain on campus with credit, but that curriculum and faculty appointments be upgraded to meet the academic requirements of that university or college where ROTC is located. The report was given to the author by Northwestern's ROTC commander; it was not a "secret" document. For a more detailed examination and a history of ROTC—university relations, see Lyons and Masland (1959); for another account of the civilianization of the military, see Janowitz (1965).

but to supplement the output of the military academies and to provide a larger reserve of officers required by an enlarged military, other means of recruiting, educating, and training young officers was needed. For this reason, the Reserves Officers' Training Corps (ROTC) was established by the National Defense Act of 1916. Army ROTC units were set up on campuses that same year; the Navy ROTC was established in 1926 (Northwestern was among the very first to set up its Navy ROTC); the Air Force ROTC in 1946. The ROTC Vitalization Act of 1964 established the present statutory basis for ROTC programs.[9]

As of 1969, ROTC units were in operation on 353 colleges or universities. These units serve approximately one hundred additional colleges through cross-registration arrangements. The Army has units on 283 campuses; the Navy on 54; and the Air Force on 174. The Army ROTC program is by far the largest as well as the oldest. In 1968-69, Army ROTC enrolled 150,982 cadets and commissioned 16,415 new officers. In 1966-67, the number was 14,000 and in 1967-68, it was some 16,000. Compared to this, West Point produced 763 officers and the Officer Candidate Schools (OCS) produced 8,549. Naval ROTC in 1968-69 had enrolled 10,760 midshipmen and commissioned 1,885 to its fleets and another 155 to the United States Marine Corps. Compared to this, about 1,000 were commissioned in the Regular Navy and 700 came from the United States Naval Academy. Air Force ROTC, the newest program, in 1968 enrolled 51,273 cadets and commissioned 4,977 second lieutenants.

One can see that ROTC provides approximately 65 percent of all Army officers commissioned in that year and 55 percent of all Navy officers. The Department of Defense in its report on ROTC (1969) found it expedient to maintain ROTC for the

---

[9] It also provided that the senior commissioned officer of the armed force concerned, who is assigned to the program at a particular school, be given the academic rank of professor. Thus, at Northwestern during the protest, the NROTC commander, Col. Frank Gibson, was allowed to sit in and vote at Faculty Senate meetings; assistant professors, who had been at NU for even three years or over, did *not* have this right.

following reasons: One, to expand the military academies would be expensive. In fact, ROTC is the least expensive way to procure officers and to a cost-conscious Pentagon, this is an important reason. It is at least five times more expensive per officer to send him to a military academy then to ROTC or OCS. Two, ROTC is more convenient and more accessible than an off-campus center such as a nearby military base. Three, ROTC is felt to be superior to OCS because it produces a better educated officer, with its blend of both civilian and military studies. It is in line with the "citizen-soldier" concept that pervades U.S. history. Four, the ROTC report felt that "insofar as critics fear 'militaristic' influence in the national defense system, opposition to ROTC is singularly inappropriate—its abolition would decrease civilian influence." And last, for the sake of national security, the nation's universities should be responsible for training officers, even private universities, since their tax-exempt status constitutes a notable government subsidy (1969:26-28).

Let us now examine why ROTC was chosen as a symbol of the technocratic society.

PROTEST: SYMBOLIC AND PRAGMATIC

When radicals made the consciousness-jump between ROTC officers being trained on campus and these same officers being used in Vietnam, Laos, and Cambodia, as well as ready to repress revolutions and protect America's economic interests abroad, then it was logical to choose it as a symbol. When comparing it to other issues which have aroused activist dissent, ROTC on campus has several expedient characteristics: (a) it is always present in a physical form since there are uniform-clad participants, open-air drills and a classroom building; (b) it affects a large enough number of students to insure adequate confrontations and interest; (c) it is an issue to the administration and faculty, both on a formal level (the Faculty Senate, the CAS decision, etc.) and on an informal level of discussion; (d) it is a question which can be legitimately debated by students and faculty; and (e) compared to other issues, it is a fresh and unsolved conflict.

These characteristics made ROTC important to Northwestern. Furthermore, every protest has its symbolic as well as its practical components. As Charles Reich (1970:325) points out:

> An object of tactics was to put messages in a language—visual, emotional, and symbolic—that would help it to be heard and understood . . . it is better to show, not tell, and some ideas require emotional preparation before they can be taken in.

Or Mark Rudd (in Avorn, 1968:290):

> During the course of the Columbia strike a whole set of symbols and slogans inevitably emerged. It is difficult for someone who wasn't there . . . or for someone who's not part of the New Left to understand these symbols and their significance. Red flags, red armbands, "Up against the wall, mother fucker," communes, all became integral parts of the strike, helped define the strike.

On one level, symbols are simply identification marks, like the V-sign or long hair. On a second level, symbols represent greater issues. Pouring blood on draft files protests the draft, the war, and killing in general. Napalm made by Dow Chemical does the same thing. Likewise, "Off ROTC" protest signifies the war, imperialism abroad, and the "militarization" of the university. Taking ROTC off campus, on one campus or even on many campuses, would not have ended the war. It was symbolic of something more. It was meant to raise consciousness of other issues, and ultimately it was meant to question the entire technocratic state, especially the military-industrial-university complex within that state.

Other issues and other protest groups are more pragmatic, yet their protest is also symbolic. In fact, *all protest made by the counterculture by Blacks, or Third World Groups are symbolic.* For example, when Black students sit-in and demand a Black studies program, that is pragmatic. It is something the university can do. So it may build a Black studies program. The protest is *symbolic* in that it signifies the plight of Blacks throughout history and throughout the land, plus it can be fuel for other issues and an impetus to other Blacks to carry out similar acts of protest. One reason why Black protest on campus is usually more successful than non-Black protest is because it is practical; university officials can do something about it. White students also are usually more successful when their proposals are practical. ROTC protest is more symbolic than practical. University officials cannot end the war or end exploitative imperialism, therefore the demands of the protest are seen as impractical and the protesters are subject to a greater chance of punishment if they insist upon them.

ROTC protesters failed in their short-range plans; ROTC remains on campus. It failed in even its long-range plans. There were several reasons: first, powerful decision-making groups, in fact *the* decision-makers, the faculty, did not agree with the radicals' contention that ROTC was an arm of United States imperialism. The radicals failed to raise consciousness to a degree in which the faculty would have agreed and would have abolished ROTC from campus; two, faculty, as well as students, were so preoccupied with the violent tactics used by radicals, that the symbolic "message" was lost, and the opposite result occurred: people began to ignore the issue of ROTC and dwelled on the tactics. These same forces operate when Blacks use the symbol "pig" and engage in battles with police. Tactics throw a "smokescreen" over issues.

CONCLUSION

What then can be said about the protest of this last decade? In large measure, it failed in elementary ways to do what it intended to do. The radical approach failed because the technocracy was too strong, too determined, and too "turned off" by style and tactics; the liberal reformistic approach failed because it saw its duties in a piecemeal fashion, to change a section here and a section there. An over-all view was missing. The war continued; ecological disasters continued; the grinding poverty of the ghetto continued. There is one alternative, though, for change. The generation of students who entered college in the early and mid-sixties is now graduating. This cohort is now, in the 1970's, entering the world outside the university. If they can begin to transform the institutions they now enter, whether it be business, the professions, or the military, and if they can, by means of a new life-style and *weltanschauung,* influence the people around them, then the protest of the 1960's was not done in vain. But it will take what European student leader Rudi Dutscke has called the "long hard march through the institutions of the society." If that occurs, then there is still hope for meaningful change in America.

REFERENCES

Avorn, Jerry L. *Up Against the Ivy Wall: A History of the Columbia Crisis.* New York: Atheneum, 1968.

Barber, Richard J. *The American Corporation.* New York: Dutton. 1970.

Birenbaum, William M. *Overlive, Power, Poverty, and the University.* New York: Dell, 1969.

Braden, William. *The Age of Aquarius: Technology and the Cultural Revolution.* Chicago: Quadrangle, 1970.

Department of Defense. Report of the Special Committee on ROTC. Washington, D.C.: Department of Defense, Manpower and Reserve Affairs, 1969.

Ellul, Jacques. *The Technological Society.* New York: Random House, 1964.

Galbraith, John Kenneth. *The New Industrial State.* New York: New American Library, 1967.

Horowitz, David. "Billion Dollar Brains." *Ramparts.* May. and "Sinews of Empire." August, 1969.

Janowitz, Morris. *Sociology and the Military Establishment.* New York: Russell Sage Foundation, 1965.

Kerr, Clark. *The Uses of the University.* New York: Harper and Row, 1963.

Lyons, Gene M. and John W. Masland. *Education and Military Leadership: A Study of ROTC.* Princeton, New Jersey: Princeton University Press, 1959.

Melman, Seymour. *Pentagon Capitalism: The Political Economy of War.* New York: McGraw-Hill, 1970.

Mesthene, Emmanuel G. *Technological Change.* New York: New American Library, 1970.

Mills, C. Wright. *The Power Elite.* New York: Oxford University Press, 1956.

Mills, C. Wright. *The Causes of World War Three.* New York: Ballantine, 1958.

Reich, Charles A. *The Greening of America.* New York: Random House, 1970.

Ridgeway, James. *The Closed Corporation: American Universities in Crisis.* New York: Ballantine, 1968.

Roszak, Theodore. *The Making of a Counter Culture: Reflections on the Technocratic Society and Its Youthful Opposition.* Garden City, New York: Doubleday (Anchor Books), 1969.

Servan-Schreiber, J. J. *The American Challenge.* New York: Atheneum, 1968.

Trebing, Harry M. (ed.) *The Corporation in the American Economy.* Chicago: Quadrangle, 1970.

Yarmolinsky, Adam. *The Military Establishment: Its Impact on American Society.* New York: Harper and Row, 1970.

Zeitlin, Maurice (ed.) *American Society, Inc.* Chicago: Markham, **1970.**

Chapter VII
Epilogue: Beyond the Protest

Society is in constant flux. To study society is by choice to introduce cloture. To study political movements, student movements being only one example, is to arbitrarily end at a particular point in time. A movement is process; a book is static.

This research "ended," in a sense, on a momentous occasion for the nation, for the university, and for ROTC: the May 1970 national student strike. The purpose of this epilogue is to update, analyze, and describe what occurred since May 1970 to May 1971. Next year another epilogue can be written, and so continued *ad infinitum*.

The first section of this chapter will deal with local university events; the one following, with national events. Though not every national event influences the university and conversely not every university and student event is a reaction to national events, it can be said that in the area of ROTC protest (which is linked so closely to anti-war, anti-draft, and anti-Vietnam protest), national and local protest co-intersect and co-influence. In other areas, for example the economic situation (the effect of the business inflation on educational institutions), there are further examples of this influence.

Generally speaking, the university can be seen as a microcosm of "white" America and reflects its failures, successes, and aspirations. As a "holding place" for nearly five percent of this nation's population, the colleges and universities may seem puny in size, but their influence is far-reaching because of their explosive concentration of knowledge, expertise, and youthful energy.

THE LOCAL SCENE: THE STUDENTS

At the beginning of the fall term, September 1970, at Northwestern as well as on many campuses across the country, the tone on the part of most students was one of disillusionment and apathy.

There was little student protest for most of the year until the "spring offensive" in 1971. NROTC was no longer an issue. This was due in part to the breakdown of NU's SDS chapter. Many of its leaders had been either suspended, expelled, or put on probation. When credit was taken away by the College of Arts and Sciences in the spring of 1970, that seemed another reason for radical students to close the issue. As one SDS member put it:

> By taking away credit (from NROTC), our job is over. They'll have to abolish it (NROTC) soon. But we've got to move on. NROTC was too high a price to pay—over 30 people were hurt, arrested, or put on probation, and that's too high a price to pay when you consider that we've ignored other issues —university expansion into the Black community, "pig" research, and even our own heads.

If the national radical movement scene was relatively "calm," so too was the local scene. The fall and winter of 1970 was a time for *reflection and re-evaluation of goals and tactics.* While SDS was quiet on campus, other groups were gaining strength: women's liberation groups, radical Jewish student groups, and student mobilization (anti-Vietnam) groups.

Even when the U.S. invaded Laos in January of 1971, only about 100 students turned out for a rally. This should be compared to the massive demonstrations following the Cambodia invasion of May 1970.

The strike at NU had profound implications for SDSers. It pointed out how an issue can "die," not by failure, but by apparent success. It pointed out the radicals' own organizational weaknesses, the difficulties with working with liberals and moderates, and it graphically showed the gap in political consciousness between radicals and other students.

The liberal student, both nationally and locally, also faced a situation that Edgar Z. Friedenberg has called *réssentement,* a kind of free-floating resentment directed somewhere "out there"—aimed at school administrators and national leaders. Such *réssentement* is fuel for future protest; it is hidden from view and, therefore, many observers see a surface calm and feel that political protest is over. This is not the case; the resentment, frustration, and disillusionment are read to emerge and crystalize into collective behavior at any moment.

Liberal students at NU were disillusioned over many issues: the "white-wash" of the presidents' commission on student protest that failed to indict the national guardsmen who killed four college students at Kent State University; the refusal on the part of the NU faculty to allow a two-week period before the November 1970 congressional elections to allow students to campaign for the candidates of their choice; the behind-the-stage maneuverings of the school administration and trustees in their choosing of a new president;[1] the increase in tuition to $2700 a year (one of the highest in the nation); and finally, of course, the ever present war in Vietnam which seemed never to end for these students.

The conservative students, small in number and led by the Young Americans for Freedom, were able to generate little support for their attempts to sue various universities for cancelling classes during the strike. At NU such a suit was threatened, but failed to materialize. Similar suits were attempted at several midwestern universities, at Washington University in St. Louis and at Ohio State University, the latter for one million dollars. As radical student protest declined or moved off-campus, counter-protest by conservative students also declined. Protest organized by such groups as YAF are "negative" protest, aimed *against* radicals, rather than "positive" protest, aimed *for* certain issues. There is a direct correlation

---

[1] For an "expose" of this search, written by one of the presidential candidates himself, see Warren Bennis' account (1971). It shows how personal and political motives (very human impulses, Bennis notes) insinuated themselves into the presidential choice—in spite of the trappings of objectivity.

between the efficaciousness of radical student protest and conservative student protest. In short, the question is not the appeal of YAF's program, but the repudiation of SDS's tactics.

As was stated, the issue of ROTC became a "dead" issue. There were no protests, no petitions, and no violence during the 1970-1971 year aimed directly at ROTC. There was, however, a referendum taken during April 1971 at the time of the school elections for student government. It offered interesting data on the change (or lack of change) in attitudes towards ROTC. Table 6 shows the difference over one year.

TABLE 6

ATTITUDES TOWARD NROTC SEEN LONGITUDINALLY

CHOICES	Student Referendum Apr. 14, 1970 (N 3,459)	Student Referendum Apr. 21, 1971 (N 2,125)
#1 Remove NROTC from campus	27%	28%
#2 NROTC should remain, but carry no credit	32%	24%
#3 NROTC should remain on campus in its present form	41%	41%
#4 NROTC should be removed from campus but carry credit	(not asked)	7%
	100%	100%
Abstentions (not included in the above N's)	433	308

The overriding import of the referendum was that there was little significant difference in attitudes toward ROTC over the year. A majority (52 percent) of the voters favored abolishing ROTC credit either by completely abolishing it or allowing it on campus but without credit. However, a plurality of voters, like the year before, 41 percent, picked the status-quo choice, No. 3. In 1971, only 24 percent favored keeping ROTC on campus, without credit, as compared to 1970's total of 32 percent. Choice No. 4 was not asked in 1970, and garnered only 7 percent of the vote. The number of abstentions was not proportionately different either year.

What conclusions can one draw? First, given the impact of the strike and the fact that there was no anti-ROTC protest by SDS during the year, the tenacity of attitudes over the year was important to note. Like the year before, one can use these statistics to back any one of many views. The issue of ROTC was still split more or less three ways.

In conclusion, one should not emerge from all this with a totally negative picture. There were more students on various university committees; there were more consultations with students and student leaders over matters of policy; there were to be some changes in the grading system; and there were proposals to erect residential colleges around living units with closer faculty-student ties.

But generally there is the feeling that the rate of change is much too slow and thus frustration grows. At Northwestern this is translated as the slowness of the school administration in its accommodation to student demands over symbolic gestures vis à vis national policy and/or over shared decision-making powers. Along with more general social conditions, it seems that this slowness, more than ever, will be important factors in demonstrative action in the future.

THE LOCAL SCENE: THE FACULTY

The year following the strike was also a time of re-evaluation for the faculty. There was also a re-evaluation of attitudes toward ROTC courses. This re-evaluation was, however, seen by a student editorial as 'vacillation, procrastination, and reversal." In short, the College of Arts and Sciences reversed itself one year after the Kent State—Cambodia strike and restored credit to four NROTC courses. Why this reversal? First, before answering that question, let us review the history of CAS faculty decision-making with regards to ROTC.

In May 1969, the CAS voted to remove the Department of Naval Science from its school, effective June 1971. They also referred the issue of credit to a committee (the Heflebower committee)—after voting as a committee-of-the-whole to take credit away from all NROTC courses. After much debate, the CAS in January 1970 voted to remove credit from all but three NROTC courses, and in a close vote, 69 to 66, also voted *not* to remove credit from *all* courses.

At the same time, the Faculty Senate appointed the special Committee on the Department of Naval Science to review credit, courses, and to help find a "new home" for the department. (This committee consisted of faculty, administrators, and students, and was called the Leopold Committee after its chairman). The Faculty Senate had voted to keep the NROTC unit on campus.

Then during the furor of the strike, the CAS voted 162 to 123 by mail ballot to remove *all* credit. Then after one year of committee work and re-evaluation, the CAS reversed itself and accepted credit for four courses. While the 1970 spring strike faculty meetings of both the Faculty Senate and the CAS were both marked by intense debate over ROTC, the 1971 meetings were quiet and nearly devoid of debate.

University President Strotz summed up the reasons for this succinctly:

> The mood prevailing at the time (of the strike) caused the removal of credit. Any social psychologist could see that.

The mood a year after the strike was one of surface calm and thus, faculty resorted to what may have been their true inclinations. The strike descended upon the campus like some sort of *deus ex machina* propelling people into action that they would not have condoned or been party to during a calmer atmosphere. The following discussion of faculty attitudes (seen in retrospect one year later), while differing in particular details, seems to be generalizable for most campus faculties across the nation.

First, professors have an image of themselves as calm, mature, and deliberate. The strike upset this image and directly "stampeded" the faculty to endorse action that many neither agreed with both in substance and in style.

As one professor in CAS put it and he seemed to speak for most:

> Many faculty felt a bit ashamed about the strike . . . it was not typical of me, I was led by emotion. Now, the emotionalism is gone; rationalism is back . . . we did the right thing because we had to do something, but I'd never do it again in the same way.

Here were a few of the issues that "turned off" professors and may explain the "backlash":

First, there was the humiliation of being "stampeded" into action. Many faculty were angry that the general faculty meeting held in May 1970 to simply discuss the strike had turned into a massive pro-strike meeting.

Second, there were, of course, professors angry about ever having a strike at all, let alone the style in which it was endorsed.

Third, there were faculty who were angered because they supported the Vietnam War and the Cambodian invasion.

Fourth, there were those who were incensed that the strike turned into a "lock-out." In this instance, there was a kind of discrimination at work: professors in the engineering, physical, and chemical sciences on the north campus were locked out of their offices and labs. (Students stood guard and barricaded the doors). But professors of humanities and social sciences on the south campus were not locked out; they could enter their offices.

Fifth, the deans of the various schools were indignant that their faculties were called for that general faculty meeting without their consent.

Sixth, the deans and a fair number of professors were vexed that the General Faculty Committee of the Faculty Senate and especially its chairman had "usurped" power and done things that either were not in their power or that should have been undertaken by the administration, e.g. voting to send a delegation of faculty and students to Washington to petition the government, committing the university to the strike (by introducing such a resolution), and by generally acting in a style that many felt was "politicizing" the university. Yet amidst such condemnation many felt that given the circumstances, such action was necessary to avoid violence and polarization.

Seventh, many faculty regretted that teaching was abandoned during the strike. Furthermore, there were those that were angry that students took advantage of the strike and simply "took off on a vacation." (Few did this.)

Eighth, many faculty were angered at the "Lunt Hall incident," wherein SDSers entered NROTC offices during the strike with the intention of non-violently moving NROTC files and furniture out of the building: this led to violence—fights and destruction of some property. (Thirty-three radical students were eventually charged with criminal damage.)

All these reasons, plus the return to "normalcy," led to the reversal of credit for NROTC courses a year later. There is one more important point to add. The strength of faculty decision-making powers is effected by economic reasons, among others. In times of prosperity and an open market, professors will be more likely to speak out on provocative issues and take more "militant" action. But in times of recession and a tight job market, professors will tend to be more cautious for fear of losing their jobs, not being rehired somewhere else, and/or not getting raises in salary (thus tenured professors are also affected). This subtle economic issue then had important impact on faculty and may partially explain the "backlash" attitudes.

THE LOCAL SCENE: THE ADMINISTRATION

The national recession of the early 1970's had an important role in influencing universities and colleges—especially private ones such as NU. It may even force private institutions to become public, or close entirely.

This crisis was acute for NU. Tuition was increased to $2700 a year, which angered any students who felt they were not getting an adequate educational return for such a heavy outlay of money, which can run to nearly $25,000 for a four-year undergraduate program including tuition, room, board, and personal expenses.

With tuition rising at schools across the country, small private colleges like NU seem to be in particular danger of pricing themselves out of business. High tuition costs can also lead to a homogenizing of the student body—with more well-to-do families being able to afford these costs while the less-well-to-do, Blacks, other minority groups, working class whites and even middle-class families unable to attend such schools.

Admissions people report an accelerating shift of enrollments from small private colleges to state universities and to low-cost community colleges close to students' homes. (Northwestern Report, 1971: 48.)

Administrators at NU are closely watching this crisis. Student protest which could lead to increased maintenance and repair costs as well as "turn off" prospective alumni and corporate donors would not be continanced for *economic* as well as the usual *political* reasons. In fact a letter sent to all prospective NU freshmen by the Chancellor Roscoe Miller touched on this very issue:

> If you have any misgivings or reservations as to your willingness to adhere to (our) rules established for the protection of the University community, you should spare yourself and the University future troubles by reconsidering your decision to enroll at Northwestern.

Besides economic issues, NU was also involved in various administrative reshuffling. A new president, Robert Strotz, former dean of the CAS at NU, was chosen. (See Bennis, 1971: 39-53.) The Northwestern Board of Trustees named three new vice-presidents to fill two newly created and one vacant administrative post. New appointees were chosen for the vice-president in charge of planning and development, the vice-president and dean of faculties, and the vice-president for science and research. A search committee was also set up to select a candidate for vice-president and dean of students, a position that is so vulnerable, being a "middleman" role between students and administration.

Because of the tensions caused by student protest, strenuous and complex committee work, and long arduous work loads, there is a great deal of job shifting and a higher turnover of administrators than in the past.

Furthermore, administrative appointees also come under fire when it is felt that certain sectors of the university are not fully consulted. For example, student leaders at NU objected to the final choice of a university president because they had not been consulted, and if consulted, then not heeded; faculty, specifically the general faculty committee, objected to the creation and filling of the post of vice-president for science and research because that post had not had faculty approval. The politics of consensus, involving *all* sectors of the university, a most difficult form of politics, is a goal still to be sought on most campuses. Out of sheer frustration, if not outright bad faith, university administrators and boards of trustees (or regents) may autocratically consolidate and tightly control dissenting faculty and students in the future.

THE NATIONAL SCENE

National policy was a major touchstone for student protest and university decision-making. The nationwide effects of the recession on educational institutions has already been described. Furthermore, the moral leadership which was so necessary was notably lacking on the part of the Nixon administration. The alternative response was rhetoric, emotional polarization, and drift. Students seemed to sense that few were listening. Hence, the "politics of frustration" emerged.

During the school year following the strike, the level of protest was low. It sprang alive during the "spring offensive" of 1971 with massive (nearly half a million participants) marches in Washington, D.C. alone. There were similar rallies during this time (late April 1971) across the country and in several foreign lands in protest of the Vietnam War.

While Northwestern participated in these anti-war rallies, the issue was Vietnam, no longer ROTC. In fact there were no anti-ROTC protests throughout the year. Yet, the impact of past protest had had its effect. Enrollment in ROTC in 1970 dropped to its lowest level since 1947, the Pentagon reported. In 1968, there were 212,470 enlistees, in 1969 a total of 155,946, and in 1970, 109,598. During that three year period, the number of colleges where participation in ROTC was *compulsory* dropped from 122 to 48. In percentage terms, enrollment dropped 33 percent for the Army, 24 percent for the Air Force, and 14 percent for the Navy. (All figures from the CCO News Notes, 1971:1.)

To counteract these trends, the armed forces resorted to new techniques: more "hip" advertising campaigns, more lenient rules regarding hair style, barracks decor, and discipline, more ROTC scholarships, shorter terms of active duty, higher pay, and other incentives. A nationwide campaign began, a kind of "greening of the military." One thought that one might "sell" young people on military service like one "sells" a corporation job.

Yet it was more likely that such reforms were only the tip of the iceberg as a means of "cooling out" dissent within the armed forces. For example, the most prominent of the anti-war protesters during the 1971 spring march on Washington were Vietnam veterans, many of them officers (usually lieutenants or lower).

Even military intelligence could not be sure that its ex-employees would keep silent. For example, a former Army intelligence agent revealed widespread espionage of both liberal and conservative, as well as of course radical groups, both on and off campuses. This touched off a national furor.

Army intelligence agents, as well as FBI and local police intelligence units, as part of a national intelligence operation, conducted investigations at Northwestern. Subversive intelligence files were established on about thirty Northwestern students and three faculty members. NU was singled out for particular attention because it was considered the most "dangerous" campus in Chicago.[2] Microfilmed copies of the files on these students and teachers are now at the Army

---

[2] This information was gained from excerpts of news stories in both the *Chicago Journalism Review* (April 1971:3-5) and the *Daily Northwestern* (Thursday, February 25, 1971: 1, 5). They were taken from the actual taped interviews with the Army agent.

Intelligence Headquarters in Maryland. Of course, SDS was investigated, but the agent went on to describe other campus groups:

> We monitored any organization which had anything at all to do with politics. This included a very small Young Socialist Alliance movement, the Student Mobilization Committee (an anti-war group), the *Daily Northwestern*, the Jewish Student Movement, Young Americans for Freedom, and (local groups) such as the Businessmen to End the War in Vietnam. (*Daily Northwestern*, 1971: 1.)

The national scene was to have other "exposés" of the military—the My Lai massacre and the subsequent courtmartial of an army officer were, however, the most prominent news. Each new story, having anything to do with the war or the military, only confused pro-Vietnam sympathies, reinforced anti-Vietnam sympathies, and angered both sides. Yet the war has had a more insidious effect. It has numbed its audience to daily atrocity and violence and it has led to feelings of despair, political impotence, and enervation.

The massive anti-war marches were attempts to repudiate this despair and once again recapture hope.

At Northwestern as well as across the nation's campuses, the issue of ROTC was "dead"; it no longer had the symbolic importance it once had. The issue was now, as it always was, the war in Vietnam, and the war was both the central issue of the past decade and the catalyst for demonstrative action in the future.

CONCLUSION: SOME NOTES ON A THEORY OF PROTEST

It is difficult to conclude a study of social protest. To conclude is to abstract, but let me end with a few notes and some tentative propositions that would be helpful in any theory of protest.

First, conflict, rather than being undesirable, is a significant factor in social life. As long as there is a scarcity of freedoms, status, and resources for man's dispersal, there will be competition and conflict over the rights and privileges to those commodities. Furthermore, particular men and women are more competent, more powerful, and more prestige-laden than others; and their positions are opposed by those without such power and prestige. Therefore, over scarce allocation of goods, and over differential rewards, inequality results leading to such phenomena as conflict.

Furthermore, every conflict reveals social structure. Or as Marshall McLuhan points out: every breakdown is a potential breakthrough. The 1929 financial crash revealed the economic structure to the entire community. The breakdown of segregation revealed the nature of racism. The generation gap revealed the nature of identity. ROTC protest revealed the links between the military and the university.

Two, protest is predicated by an underlying and growing distrust of authority. Those who distrust school administrators are likely to support student protesters, and those who trust the administrators are more likely to not support the protesters.[3] This distrust of authority goes deeper. As William Graham Sumner has put it: the moment the mores are questioned, they have lost their authority. Distrust of authority can lead to rejection of that authority. And when mores are questioned publicly by public figures of an institution (let us say, for example, prominent professors), then they not only have lost their authority, but are ready to be replaced.

Three, as mores are questioned and replaced, then expectations rise and include ever more mores. Rising expectations plus frustrated goals lead to a form of relative deprivation, which in turn can lead to a "snowball" effect of protest followed by more protest. The effects of relative deprivation holds true not only for oppressed minority groups such as Afro-Americans or Chicanos, but for women, professionals, union members, army personnel, and students as well. Furthermore, as a relatively privileged and educated class such as college students, or better yet, youth generally, attempts to emulate and adopt the life-styles of the poor and the oppressed, then

---

[3] This is supported by evidence cited in Kornhauser (1971:266-268).

that privileged class incorporates the frustrations of the oppressed class. In any case, relative deprivation leads to accelerated conflict which leads to accelerated social change.

Four, social change caused by *student* protest is only one example of social change within the society. The university is only one setting. There are other significant sectors of the off-campus protest movement, much of it less publicized: young radicals in the professions—recent graduates of universities who have gone into teaching, urban planning, law, medicine, social work, and other fields, being a prime example. Other areas that are fertile ground for movement expansion are the armed forces, prisons, labor unions, and non-unionized workers. Such expansion will spread the base of change: the universities will no longer be a central base of operations.

Fifth, the dialectical interplay between social being and social consciousness is a crucial feature of history. For the most part, the cultural changes produced by this tension have been gradual. However, in an era of advanced technological development, the process of significant structural change proceeds at a dramatically accelerated pace in a technocratic society.

And what has been called the "cultural revolution" in America today is fundamentally the development of a complex of new social and personal values which emanate from—and are much more suitable to—an America which has changed more in the past 25 years than it did in the previous one hundred.

The political revolt is aimed at the structure of power and privilege; the cultural revolt is aimed at the mores and traditions of society. In America, at the present time, the two are intertwined and inter-dependent.

In every area of cultural and social life—education, religion, art, philosophy, politics, life goals, life-styles—old, established ideas have been questioned, attacked, and rejected by significant, and growing, sectors of the population.

Attitudes toward work, career, money, interpersonal relationships—a set of values which once comprised the basic cultural codification of American life—have clearly lost their hold over a sizable portion of the under-30 generation and have in some measure lost the unquestioning respect and fidelity of vast numbers of Americans in general.

Finally, let me say a few words about revolution. The term is used in a variety of ways.[4] Some equate revolution with any profound social and political change. Some with a "storming of the palace" form of *coup d'état*. Others in a more restrictive sense use the term to mean an attack on the moral-political order and the traditional hierarchy of class statuses and succeeds when existing structures lose their legitimacy and can no longer function without widescale repression.

The concept of revolution is very broad and this short discussion will not do it justice, but the question remains: something is going on—what is it?

To answer that is to write a whole new book, or a few hundred more books. But in short, what is going on is a long-term concerted political and economic action combined with innovative cultural change—revolutionizing the way people live in their daily lives and the way they relate intimately with each other. According to scholars such as Howard Zinn, this is not revolution in the true historic meaning of the term, but a slow drive for radical change using both traditional and novel means. Or as radical theoretician Richard Flacks (1971: 259) has described it:

> The revolution in advanced capitalist society is not a single insurrection. It is not a civil war of pitched battles fought by opposing armies. It is a long, continuing struggle—with political, social, and cultural aspects inextricably intertwined. It is already underway. It is not simply a socialist revolution, if by that one means the establishment of a new form of state power . . . It is more than that. For it must be a revolution in which the power to make key decisions is placed in the hands of those whose lives are determined by those decisions. It is, in short, not a revolution aimed at seizing power but a revolution aimed at its dispersal.

---

[4] For a fine summary of the term, see Lasch (1971:318-334).

It would be best to conclude with a few words from Karl Marx: to be radical is to grasp the matter by its root. Now the root of mankind is man himself, and the real meaning of revolution is not a change in management, but a change in man. The purpose of social protest is to effectuate such a change.

Nineteenth century ideologies (particularly Marxism) which arose as a reaction to an industrializing European society have been exhausted in the twentieth century. What is necessary is a re-evaluation and reformulation of theories of change that are suitable to a complex post-industrial technocracy. Such a reformulation would lead to both theory and *praxis*. It is still in the process of being formulated.

REFERENCES

Bennis, Warren. "Searching for the 'Perfect' University President." *The Atlantic*, 227 (April): 39-53, 1971.

CCCO News Notes. "ROTC in Trouble." Philadelphia: Center for the Committee of Conscientious Objectors. 23 (January): 1, 1971.

Chicago Journalism Review. "Army Spies and the Press." (April): 3-5, 1971.

Flacks, Richard. "Revolt of the Young Intelligentsia: Revolutionary Class-Consciousness in a Post-Scarcity America." Pp. 223-259 in Roderick Aya and Normal Miller (eds.). *The New American Revolution.* New York: Free Press, 1971.

Kornhauser, William. "The Politics of Confrontation." Pp. 264-283 in Roderick Aya and Normal Miller (eds.). *The New American Revolution.* New York: Free Press, 1971.

Lasch, Christopher. "Epilogue." Pp. 318-334 in Roderick Aya and Norman Miller (eds.). *The New American Revolution.* New York: Free Press, 1971.

Northwestern Daily. "Army Agent Gives NU Spy Details." 91 (Thursday, February 25): 1, 5, 1971.

Northwestern Report. "Small-School Troubles." Northwestern Report 2 (Winter): 48, 1971.